THE
BOLSA CHICA
GUN CLUB

THE
BOLSA CHICA
GUN CLUB

A HISTORY

Chris Epting

THE
History
PRESS

Published by The History Press
Charleston, SC
www.historypress.com

Cover images:
Front, top left: (*Left to right*) Marcus McCallen (Huntington Beach City Council, 1938–42; there's a park in Huntington Beach named after him), Edna Cooper, Billy McCallen and Huntington Beach police chief Les Grant, circa the early 1930s. *Author's collection.*
Front, top middle: The Bolsa Chica Gun Club in the early 1930s. Note the pristine front lawn. *Huntington Library.*
Front, top right: Gun club member, possibly H. Lee Borden, near the boat launch in 1902. *Author's collection.*
Front, bottom: A family poses in front of the gun club, circa 1905. *Author's collection.*
Back: Guests arriving at the Bolsa Chica Gun Club, circa 1903. *Author's collection.*
Back, inlay: Henry Huntington. *Author's collection.*

First published 2024

Manufactured in the United States

ISBN 9781467150439

Library of Congress Control Number: 2023950469

This book is dedicated to Dennis McGirk,
the farmer who fought the millionaires.

If the air feels thick
If shadows appear
If time seems to wrinkle
There's nothing to fear
It may just be layers
Of people and past
That once were right here
Where memories last
The space where you wander
Though just walking through
May still hold the ghosts
that hold onto you

—Chris Epting

CONTENTS

Preface   11
Acknowledgements   15

1. Gun Clubs in Orange County   17
2. The Pacific Flyway and Native Americans   23
3. A Gun Club Is Born   28
4. How the Club Was Run   33
5. Tom Talbert   36
6. Life at the Bolsa Chica Gun Club   39
7. Shooting Logs, Maps, Bylaws and Meeting Notes   54
8. Members, Guests and Workers   61
9. The Birth of Huntington Beach and the Red Cars
        That Arrived   83
10. Farm-to-Table Sustainability   88
11. The War with the Farmers   92
12. How Huntington Beach Viewed the Club   97
13. The Press   100
14. Hubert Latham   105
15. Oil!   113
16. The Bolsa Chica Gun Club on Film   117
17. The Military   121
18. The Transformation of the Bolsa Chica Gun Club   125
19. Ownership   130

CONTENTS

20. "Smoky" Stevens   136
21. A Survey and Then a Win for the Farmers   142
22. A Walk Today   147
23. Is Anything Left?   153
24. Who Takes Care of the Area Today?   163

Afterword: What's Next?   169
Bibliography   171
About the Author   173

PREFACE

As a writer, a storyteller and a historian, I have always been captivated by the hidden tales that lie beneath the surface of the world around us. It is these untold narratives, the whispers of forgotten history, that beckon me forward and fuel my insatiable curiosity. One such story, which I stumbled upon after first moving to Huntington Beach in 1999, has since consumed many waking thoughts—the enigmatic and mythical Bolsa Chica Gun Club.

It all began innocently enough. As a newcomer to this coastal paradise in 1999, I found solace and tranquility in the sprawling beauty of the Bolsa Chica Wetlands. Avidly exploring its trails, I reveled in the symphony of nature's melodies, accompanied by the gentle rustling of grasses, flowers and the distant call of migrating birds. Yet it was amid this serene backdrop that I first caught wind of whispered tales, stories that spoke of a secretive and exclusive gun club, shrouded in mystery and steeped in history.

It was a comma in the fabric of my perception, a pause in the rhythm of my walks, that brought these stories to my attention. As my gaze wandered beyond the vibrant tapestry of palm and eucalyptus trees, it settled on a fenced-off portion of the wetlands. There, amid the lush greenery, stood the hallowed former grounds of the Bolsa Chica Gun Club—an oasis reserved for a chosen few, concealed from the prying eyes of the outside world.

In that moment, an insatiable hunger for knowledge took hold of me. I became consumed by a burning desire to unearth the truth behind this hidden enclave, to peel back the layers of time and reveal the forgotten stories that lay dormant within its walls. For it was clear; it was my duty, my calling, to bring to light the full tale of the Bolsa Chica Gun Club.

It's hard not to be captivated by the history of this site. I can't help but wonder what conversations were had, what deals were made and what decisions were taken that have had a lasting impact on the growth of Southern California. The air is thick with the ghosts of the past, and it feels as though the whispers of former club members still echo faintly in the breeze.

The final remnants of the club are now being slowly reclaimed by the surrounding vegetation, a poignant reminder of the fleeting nature of power and prestige.

The site of the Bolsa Chica Gun Club may be overgrown and abandoned, but it still holds a special place in the history of Southern California. It's a place that evokes a sense of mystery and wonder, a place that reminds us of the power of the past to shape the present. As a writer, I am grateful for the opportunity to explore this site and to let my imagination run wild as I try to uncover the stories that are waiting to be told.

It's intriguing to observe how certain legendary local locations, such as the Golden Bear nightclub, the Surf Theater, the Carnegie Library and the Pav a Lon Ballroom, have managed to maintain a level of recognition and awareness over time. However, it's interesting to note that the Bolsa Chica Gun Club seems to have eluded widespread knowledge and recognition, despite its historical significance.

One possible reason for this disparity is the gun club's geographical location. Situated several miles away from the downtown area, it resided on the upper mesa within the isolated wetlands of Huntington Beach. This natural seclusion contributed to the club's air of mystery, making it less accessible and known to the general public.

IN CONTRAST, THE OTHER legendary locations mentioned were more centrally located, making them easily accessible and frequented by a larger number of people. Their proximity to popular areas and their involvement in cultural or entertainment scenes may have contributed to their greater recognition and remembrance.

Unlike the other well-known locations, the gun club was not easily accessible or frequented by the general public. Its distant location in the wetlands, away from popular areas, made it less visible and less known to many. Consequently, it remained shrouded in obscurity, even among those who have lived in Huntington Beach for years.

However, I find this obscurity captivating. The fact that even locals have limited knowledge about the Bolsa Chica Gun Club adds to its allure. It's this mystique and untold story that compelled me to write a book about it. I wanted to dig deeper and uncover the forgotten tales, the history and the significance of this hidden gem.

As I embark on this journey, conducting interviews and delving into archives, I hope to shed light on the gun club's past. I want to reveal the memories and experiences of those involved, capturing the essence of what it was truly like. The untold stories of the Bolsa Chica Gun Club deserve to be shared and remembered.

In the pages that follow, I invite you to join me on a journey through time—a journey that will take us back to 1899, when the foundations of the club were laid, and carry us through the ebbs and flows of its storied existence. Together, we will navigate the labyrinthine corridors of secrecy and privilege, unearthing the triumphs and tragedies, the legends and lore that have shaped this mythical sanctuary.

Prepare to be captivated, for the story that unfolds is one of intrigue, passion and the relentless pursuit of an exclusive brotherhood. As we delve into the depths of the Bolsa Chica Gun Club's history, I hope to not only satisfy your curiosity but also ignite within you the same flame of wonder and fascination that has driven me to embark on this quest. Let us embark together on this extraordinary journey, as we uncover the secrets of the Bolsa Chica Gun Club.

ACKNOWLEDGEMENTS

I would like to express my deepest gratitude to the Claremont Colleges and Library for their invaluable support and extensive resources. The wealth of knowledge accessible through their libraries and the assistance provided by their staff have been instrumental in the research and creation of this work.

I extend my sincere appreciation to Dave Carlberg and Luann Murray for their unwavering support and guidance throughout the entire process. Their expertise and insights have greatly enriched the content of this book, and I am truly grateful for their contributions.

I would also like to acknowledge the Bolsa Chica Conservancy for its significant role in preserving the natural beauty and ecological integrity of the Bolsa Chica wetlands. Its commitment to environmental conservation has inspired me, and I am honored to be an advisory board member of such a remarkable organization.

Furthermore, I extend my heartfelt thanks to Tamara Asaki for her invaluable assistance and support. Her dedication and contributions have been indispensable, and I am grateful for her involvement in this project.

To all the individuals, organizations and institutions who have contributed to this work in various ways, I am indebted to your collective help and support. Your contributions have enriched the depth and quality of this endeavor, and I am truly grateful for your assistance. Of course, thank you to the entire team at The History Press, especially my editors, Laurie Krill and Ashley Hill.

Lastly, I would like to thank my family, friends and loved ones for their unwavering support and understanding throughout the process of researching and writing this book. Your encouragement and belief in me have been the driving force behind its completion, and I am forever grateful for your presence in my life.

1

GUN CLUBS IN ORANGE COUNTY

L et's first set the stage. By the turn of the twentieth century, Orange County, California, had gained a reputation as a sportsman's paradise, offering a diverse range of hunting opportunities. The region had become known for not only its abundant waterfowl populations but also for other game species, such as quail, pigeon, rabbit, deer, bear, coyote and bobcat.

Orange County's favorable geographical features and natural habitats contributed to its appeal as a hunting destination. The county boasted a varied landscape, including coastal wetlands, grasslands, chaparral-covered hills and oak woodlands. These diverse ecosystems provided suitable habitats for an array of game species, attracting hunters from near and far.

Waterfowl hunting was particularly popular in Orange County, thanks to its extensive wetland areas. The county's marshes, ponds and lakes attracted large numbers of migratory waterfowl, including ducks and geese. Hunters flocked to these wetlands, taking advantage of the rich hunting opportunities presented by the annual waterfowl migrations.

In addition to waterfowl, Orange County offered excellent hunting for upland game species. Quail, known for their challenging flight and elusive nature, were prevalent in the county's grasslands and brushy areas. Pigeon hunting was another favored pursuit, with large flocks of these birds often found in agricultural fields and open spaces.

Orange County's diverse wildlife extended beyond birds to include mammals. The presence of deer, bear, coyote and bobcat added to the allure of the region for sportsmen. The county's rugged hills and forests provided ideal habitats for these animals, allowing for exciting hunting experiences.

The abundance of game in Orange County during this era can be attributed to several factors. The county's relatively undeveloped landscape and the presence of large tracts of open land provided ample space for wildlife populations to thrive. Additionally, hunting regulations and practices of the time were generally less restrictive compared to modern conservation efforts, allowing for more extensive hunting opportunities.

As a result, Orange County attracted hunting enthusiasts who sought to pursue a variety of game species. The county's combination of diverse habitats, plentiful game populations and sense of adventure made it an appealing destination for hunters in the early twentieth century.

Dozens of hunting clubs were established along the immediate coastline, with at least twenty-six hunting and fishing clubs in the Anaheim/Sunset Bay Wetlands alone. These clubs catered to the interests of hunters, who sought opportunities to pursue highly regarded game birds found in the wetlands. Waterfowl, such as ducks and geese, were particularly sought after by hunters due to their abundance and sporting value.

The establishment of hunting clubs in the region not only provided recreational opportunities but also reflected the importance of wetlands as a habitat for game birds. The popularity of hunting in these wetlands underscored the rich biodiversity and availability of game birds that were valued for their sporting qualities and as a food source.

As well, the influence of the military cannot be overlooked. During this period, the United States was involved in several conflicts, including the Spanish-American War and World War I. Military training and discipline were highly valued, and many gun club members were veterans or active members of the military. Shooting clubs provided a way for these individuals to continue their training and maintain their marksmanship skills, even when they were not on active duty.

Another reason for the popularity of gun clubs in Orange County during this time was the desire for social interaction. Shooting clubs provided a venue for individuals to gather and socialize with like-minded people. Members of gun clubs often held social events, such as banquets and picnics, which provided opportunities for members to get to know each other outside of shooting competitions. Many of these social events were quite elaborate, with fine food, music and other entertainment, and they provided a way for members to connect and build lasting friendships.

In addition to these factors, the popularity of gun clubs in Orange County can also be attributed to the culture of the time. The late 1800s and early 1900s were times of rapid industrialization and urbanization, and people were increasingly disconnected from nature and the outdoors. Shooting clubs provided a way for people to reconnect with the natural world and to engage in an activity that required skill and precision. Shooting clubs also provided a way for people to escape the stresses of modern life and to find a sense of camaraderie with others who shared their interests.

It is important to note, however, that the popularity of gun clubs in Orange County during this time was not without controversy. Some people saw the proliferation of shooting clubs as a threat to public safety, and there were concerns about accidents and injuries. In addition, there were fears that the popularity of shooting clubs would lead to the depletion of wildlife populations. These concerns led to increased regulation of shooting clubs and hunting activities in the area.

In the late nineteenth century, the San Joaquin Marsh, located just upstream from the Newport Bay in California, was a renowned destination for duck hunting. James Irvine II, owner of the expansive Irvine Ranch, included the marsh as part of his vast landholding. Alongside Irvine, Count Jaro von Schmidt, a wealthy, enigmatic Austrian count and prominent Los Angeles businessman and sportsman, played a significant role in the hunting activities in the area.

During this time, von Schmidt and Irvine collaborated and established the San Joaquin Gun Club, a duck hunting club that catered to the interests of sportsmen in the region. The club provided a gathering place for hunting enthusiasts, who would convene at the marsh, engage in their beloved sport and socialize with one another. The San Joaquin Gun Club became a prominent hub for these activities.

However, toward the end of the century, a disagreement arose between James Irvine and the club members, resulting in a falling out. This discord left the hunters without a place to pursue their passion for duck hunting and deprived them of the camaraderie they had enjoyed at the San Joaquin Marsh.

Recognizing the predicament faced by these displaced sportsmen, particularly those from Los Angeles and Pasadena, von Schmidt took it upon himself to find an alternative location where they could continue their hunting pursuits and maintain their social connections. Drawing upon his connections and resources, von Schmidt embarked on a quest to discover a new site suitable for hunting that would also serve as a gathering spot for the community.

Prior to the close of the nineteenth century, the coastline between San Pedro and Newport Beach was adorned with over 17,000 acres of lush

Count Jaro von Schmidt. *Author's collection.*

wetlands. Among these wetlands, a significant portion, approximately 2,300 acres, belonged to Abel Stearns's extensive 8,100-acre Rancho La Bolsa Chica. In the final decades of the 1800s, parcels of the Rancho La Bolsa Chica were being snatched up by eager Yankee farmers, but interestingly, there were no takers for the wetland areas of the ranch. These marshlands were generally perceived as worthless.

However, news of the availability of the Bolsa Chica Wetlands reached the ears of von Schmidt, who was accompanied by the group of former members of the San Joaquin Marsh Club. Recognizing the potential value, they banded together and established the Bolsa Land Company in 1899. With a sum of $25,000, the company successfully acquired approximately 1,160 acres of the wetlands. Subsequently, they formed the Bolsa Chica Gun Club, which leased the newly acquired Bolsa Chica lands from the Bolsa Land Company for a mere $1 per year. Von Schmidt assumed the role of the inaugural club president, leading the way for their endeavors.

In the early 1990s, Louann Murray, a respected writer, environmentalist and longtime resident of Huntington Beach, penned a captivating article for *Orange Coast* magazine. The focus of her piece was the Bolsa Chica Gun Club, delving into its intriguing history and impact on the local community. Murray's insights on the club still add valuable perspective.

> *Back in the day when prominent Pasadena and Los Angeles businessmen, including von Schmidt, sought a location to establish their own exclusive gun club, the Bolsa Chica Mesa stood as a remote and isolated bluff. It overlooked a saline marsh, nourished by the freshwater currents of Freeman Creek, which flowed adjacent to the Bolsa Chica Mesa after originating from a spring in Westminster. With the acquisition of the property from Abel Stearns, these entrepreneurs possessed the power to set their own rules within this secluded sanctuary. The club swiftly became a gathering place for the uber-wealthy elite of that era.*

And who exactly was Stearns, and how did he acquire the property?

Abel Stearns

Abel Stearns was a pioneer ranch owner and businessman in Los Angeles with a fascinating life and career. He faced early hardships, having been orphaned in 1810, which led him to leave his native Massachusetts and embark on a seafaring journey. Stearns traveled extensively, making voyages to China, the East Indies and Latin America. By the early 1820s, he returned to the United States and endeavored to establish himself as a businessman, primarily dealing in shoes.

In 1826, Stearns set his sights on Mexico and settled in its capital, Mexico City. There, he became a partner in a colonization enterprise for Upper California, which eventually led to his naturalization as a Mexican citizen. In 1829, he relocated to Monterey, California, while awaiting approval of a land grant. During this time, he engaged in merchandising to sustain himself.

Around 1833, Stearns made Los Angeles his permanent home. He joined forces with Juan Bandini in the trading business and married Bandini's daughter Arcadia. Stearns became involved in a wide range of businesses and held various minor political offices. In 1849, he was chosen as a representative of the Los Angeles district in the state constitutional convention held in Monterey.

Throughout his life, Stearns began acquiring extensive ranch properties, amassing vast landholdings and cattle by 1858. His entrepreneurial spirit, involvement in politics and successful ventures contributed significantly to the growth and development of the Los Angeles region during that era. Abel Stearns's legacy as a prominent figure in the early history of Los Angeles remains notable to this day.

The upland parcels of Abel Stearns's Rancho La Bolsa Chica were in high demand among Yankee farmers. These parcels, located away from the wetland areas, were considered valuable for agricultural purposes. However, the wetland portions of the ranch did not attract any potential buyers. This was primarily because the land was perceived as worthless marshland with little economic potential.

After thorough exploration and careful consideration, von Schmidt realized he had found the ideal location. This new site, which possessed abundant waterfowl and offered a similar environment to the San Joaquin Marsh, would serve as a haven for the displaced sportsmen. It provided them with an opportunity to resume their cherished pastime and reconnect with their fellow hunting enthusiasts.

Jaro von Schmidt knew he had struck gold. But what about the history of the area? What else made it so special?

2

THE PACIFIC FLYWAY
AND NATIVE AMERICANS

L et's take a step back for a moment. What else made this area so appealing? The Bolsa Chica Wetlands, like many other regions in California, happens to lie within the Pacific Flyway. The Pacific Flyway is one of the major migratory routes followed by birds during their biannual flights between northern latitudes and tropical America. This flyway serves as a vital corridor for numerous bird species, facilitating their movement and providing essential stopover points for rest and refueling during long-distance journeys.

Native Americans

It's important at this point to recognize the history of this area to create some deeper context on just where the Bolsa Chica Gun Club sat. The club was established in 1899. But the human history of the area goes back thousands of years, more specifically between about eight and ten thousand years.

This beautiful estuary served as the ancestral homeland of Native Americans dating back as far as nine thousand years, believed to have migrated across the Bering Land Bridge. Unfortunately, little is known about these early inhabitants due to the destruction of archaeological sites caused by flooding and human activities. Over time, tribes began to establish themselves, and the principal tribes residing at Bolsa Chica were known as the Tongva and the Acjachemen. They lived in seasonal settlements on the mesa, taking advantage of the mild coastal climate to escape the harsh winters of

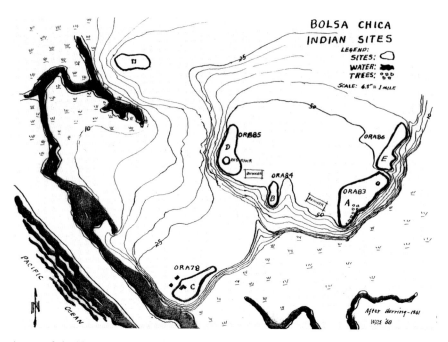

A map of significant Native American sites on and around the gun club property. *From the Pacific Coast Archaeological Society Quarterly (July 1968).*

the Santa Ana Mountains. They constructed reed and grass hemispherical huts known as wickiups or wigwams and sustained themselves by gathering resources from the land. Proficient in hunting and gathering, they excelled in crafting fine canoes for fishing and traveling to the nearby Catalina Island. They were also known for their expertise in crafting intricate baskets, which they used for a variety of purposes, including carrying food and water, storing belongings and decorating. Additionally, they created beautiful pottery and other forms of art, which were highly prized by neighboring tribes and later by European settlers.

Like the early inhabitants, little physical evidence remains at this site from these tribes, with the exception of a few burial sites, shell deposits and an archaeological treasure: cog stones.

COG STONES

The mysterious cog stones found in the Bolsa Chica Wetlands of Huntington Beach have been the subject of speculation and debate for many years. These unusual artifacts, created by the Tongva and the Acjachemen, are circular stones with a series of indentations or "cogs" carved into their surface. While their origin and purpose remain a mystery, they have captured the imagination of historians, archaeologists and laypeople alike.

The first cog stones were discovered in the Bolsa Chica Wetlands in the early 1900s, and since then, more than two hundred have been found in the area. They range in size from a few inches in diameter to several feet, and they are made from a variety of materials, including sandstone, granite and basalt.

One of the most intriguing aspects of the cog stones is their design. The cogs are evenly spaced and have a consistent size and shape, suggesting they were intentionally carved into the stones rather than the result of natural erosion or wear. Some of the stones also have additional markings, such as lines or spirals, which add to their enigmatic nature.

Many theories have been proposed to explain the purpose of the cog stones. Some have suggested that they were used as tools for grinding or crushing materials, while others have proposed that they were used in a game or some kind of ritual. Still, others have suggested that they were part of a larger mechanical device, such as a water wheel or a clock.

A cog stone discovered near the gun club location. *Author's collection.*

A cog stone discovered near the gun club location. *Author's collection.*

One of the most widely accepted theories is that the cog stones were used in some kind of agricultural context. Some have suggested that they were used as a kind of plow, with the cogs helping break up the soil and prepare it for planting. Others have proposed that they were used to grind seeds or other plant materials.

However, this theory is not without its detractors. Some have argued that the cogs would have been too small to effectively break up the soil and that there is little evidence of widespread agriculture in the area during the time that the cog stones were likely to have been used. Others have noted that the cog stones are found in such a wide variety of sizes and materials that it is unlikely that they were all used for the same purpose.

Another theory is that the cog stones were part of some kind of navigational aid or map. Some have suggested that the cogs represent a series of constellations or landmarks and that they were used to guide travelers through the area. Others have proposed that they were used to mark the locations of important resources, such as water sources or food caches.

Despite the many theories that have been proposed, the true purpose of the cog stones remains a mystery. While some progress has been made in understanding their origins, there is still much that we do not know about these enigmatic artifacts. Nevertheless, their discovery has helped shed light on the rich history of the Huntington Beach area and has inspired ongoing research and investigation.

In recent years, efforts have been made to preserve and protect the cog stones and other artifacts found in the Bolsa Chica Wetlands. The area has been designated as an ecological reserve, and efforts are underway to restore the wetlands to their natural state. At the same time, archaeologists and historians continue to study the cog stones and other artifacts found in the area, hoping to unlock the secrets of their origin and purpose.

The cog stones found in the Bolsa Chica Wetlands of Huntington Beach are fascinating and mysterious artifacts that have captured the imagination of researchers and the public alike. Despite many theories and hypotheses put forward to explain their purpose, the true role of the cog stones remains a mystery. Nevertheless, their discovery has helped shed light on the rich history of the Huntington Beach area and the broader region of Southern California. The ongoing study of these enigmatic artifacts is an important part of efforts to better understand the many diverse cultures and communities that have inhabited the area over the centuries. By preserving and studying these artifacts, we can gain a deeper appreciation for the complex and fascinating history of the region and the many contributions that its diverse peoples have made to the world. With that historic context of the area in place, we now return to history of the Bolsa Chica Gun Club.

3

A GUN CLUB IS BORN

In 1899, again, when news of the availability of the Bolsa Chica Wetlands reached Jaro von Schmidt and a group of former San Joaquin Marsh Club members, they recognized the untapped duck hunting potential of the Bolsa Chica Wetlands. They formed the Bolsa Land Company to acquire and develop the wetlands. The company aimed to transform the marshy area into a prime hunting ground for waterfowl.

Jaro von Schmidt, being instrumental in the formation of the gun club and the development of the wetlands, became its first president. His leadership and vision played a crucial role in shaping the early stages of the Bolsa Chica Gun Club and the transformation of the previously undervalued wetlands into a renowned hunting destination.

When the Bolsa Chica Gun Club opened its doors in 1899, membership came with a hefty price tag. Prospective members were required to pay an initiation fee of $1,000. This significant sum was a considerable investment for the time and served as a barrier to entry for all but the most affluent individuals (today, that would be approximately $36,000).

In addition to the initiation fee, members were also responsible for semiannual payments of sixty dollars. This ongoing financial commitment ensured the club's operational expenses were covered and helped maintain the club's facilities and amenities.

Members of the Bolsa Chica Gun Club could be subject to an annual assessment fee of $500. This fee was utilized for improvements to the club's infrastructure and the acquisition of special purchases, enhancing the overall experience for its members.

Top: The Bolsa Chica Gun Club, just after opening in 1900. *Author's collection.*

Bottom: Work on the dam begins in the early 1900s. *Author's collection.*

The club's exclusivity was reinforced by the board of directors' decision to limit membership to a total of forty men and their families. This restriction created an atmosphere of exclusivity and camaraderie among the members.

The invitation to join the Bolsa Chica Gun Club was extended solely to individuals who held stock in the Bolsa Land Company. This requirement further narrowed the pool of prospective members, ensuring that only those with a financial stake in the company were eligible to join the club.

The Bolsa Chica Gun Club, in 1899, was an expensive and exclusive establishment. The high initiation fee, recurring payments, assessment fees

Above: Members arrive at the club, circa 1902. *Author's collection.*

Opposite, top: Guests arrive at the gun club, circa 1904. *Author's collection.*

Opposite, bottom: The Bolsa Chica Gun Club as it looked around 1902. *Author's collection.*

and limited membership criteria made it accessible to only a select group of affluent individuals who were invested in the Bolsa Land Company.

Also, von Schmidt took an active role in promoting the gun club and attracting potential members to invest in its future property. To showcase the land's potential and convince people of its value, he organized trips for interested individuals. These trips were designed to provide a firsthand experience of the property and its surroundings.

Interested individuals would typically take the train from Pasadena or Los Angeles to Santa Ana. From there, they would continue their journey by

boarding a buckboard, which was a type of horse-drawn carriage or wagon. The team of horses would then transport them to the bluff, the location earmarked for the gun club.

Upon the visitors' arrival at the bluff, Count Jaro von Schmidt would personally greet them. He would enthusiastically share his vision and plans for the land, emphasizing that it would be developed into a duck club. The count would express his desire for the guests to join the club and become members, highlighting the potential benefits and returns associated with the investment.

By physically bringing potential members to the property, von Schmidt aimed to showcase the natural beauty of the area, its suitability for a duck club and the potential for future development. This approach allowed potential investors to experience the site firsthand and make informed decisions based on their observations and the count's persuasive pitches.

The *Los Angeles Evening Express* newspaper, in its edition dated October 19, 1899, could hardly contain its excitement as it announced the much-anticipated formal opening of the Bolsa Chica Gun Club. The article described it as the "best quarters in Southern California," with a new clubhouse that stood as "one of the most impressive structures in the entire state, if not the most impressive." The shooting days at the Bolsa Chica Gun Club were revealed to be Mondays, Tuesdays, Fridays and Saturdays. The formal opening of the Bolsa Chica Gun Club was described as one of the most monumental events of the year. What kind of rules helped shape the club? Let's explore that next.

4

HOW THE CLUB WAS RUN

The Bolsa Chica Gun Club was renowned for its commitment to adhering to federal and state regulations regarding hunting licenses and bag limits. As a prestigious establishment, the club upheld the highest standards in hunting practices, operating under the strict rules reminiscent of a royal Austrian hunting lodge. The entire operation was overseen by President von Schmidt, who took great care in ensuring that all members followed the established protocols.

One of the fundamental aspects of the club's regulations revolved around the gauge and types of guns permitted for use. The club strictly enforced guidelines that promoted safe and responsible hunting practices. Members were expected to use appropriate gauges and firearms that complied with the designated rules. These regulations were in place to ensure the safety of both the hunters and wildlife on the reserve.

In addition to firearm regulations, the club implemented a limited shooting schedule at the Bolsa Chica Reserve. Shooting activities were restricted to two designated days each week. This schedule allowed for the conservation and preservation of the natural habitat and ensured that hunting activities were conducted in a controlled manner.

The Bolsa Chica Gun Club gained widespread recognition for the exceptional quality of its shooting opportunities. The reserve boasted an abundance of game, making it common for members to reach their bag limits before noon. The skill and proficiency of the club's members, combined with the plentiful wildlife, contributed to a rewarding hunting experience.

This page, top: A family poses in front of the gun club, circa 1905. *Author's collection.*

This page, bottom: Guests arriving at the Bolsa Chica Gun Club, circa 1903. *Author's collection.*

Opposite: A mother and children at the beach near the Bolsa Chica Gun Club, circa 1905. *Author's collection.*

For those members who opted to extend their stay in the afternoon, the club offered a unique and luxurious amenity. Gourmet lunches were delivered directly to the blinds, allowing hunters to indulge in a fine dining experience while enjoying the tranquil surroundings of the reserve. This

attention to detail and commitment to member satisfaction further elevated the reputation of the Bolsa Chica Gun Club.

One notable development in the club's efforts occurred in May 1899, when construction began on a large dam equipped with tied gates. This dam was constructed to control the ebb and flow of tides through the natural sea opening of the wetlands. By managing the water flow, the club aimed to encourage the presence of freshwater fowl, which were believed to have more desirable taste qualities compared to saltwater fowl.

The problem was, it deprived the farmers access to the Freeman Creek and created environmental chaos. A local Orange County pioneer was brought in to help the gun club achieve what it was looking for in terms of getting the dam project completed.

5

TOM TALBERT

I n his early-1950s memoir titled *My First 60 Years in California*, Orange County pioneer Tom Talbert wrote about his efforts to help shape the gun club property after being hired by its members. In Huntington Beach particularly, Talbert remains an icon, someone who helped shape Orange County and more specifically had a hand in the early development of Huntington Beach.

In his own words:

About the years 1899 to 1900 the sportsman and hunters had become familiar with this wonderful game refuge and began organizing clubs to buy land. They bought most of the land along the coast forming about 23 or more gun clubs in almost inaccessible places. The hunters drove in through Westminster, working their way through the swabs to their respective clubs as best they could.

The Bolsa Chica Gun Club was one of the first gun clubs to operate on the coast of Southern California. The standard value of land was at this time about $20 per acre. In 1895 the club applied to the state for permission to reclaim the salt water marshlands of the bay, for, at this time, the tide extended far inland into the upper bay. The concession was granted under the state Tideland Overflow and Reclamation Act, which was the only way in which the club could acquire title to the tidelands.

By closing the channel, the land could be reclaimed for agricultural purposes. The club at once set about the task of draining and reclaiming the salty tidelands. The right to close this natural tide channel to the ocean is still questioned. An old bachelor, Mr. Farrell, and his two old maid sisters, all well up in their 60s have been working for me on the ranch. They were congenial, interesting itinerants who had traveled and worked all over the United States. I got behind with their wages and had to earn some money to pay them off before I let them go. They were loathe to leave, but I could not afford to keep them hence I was glad to get the work on the Bolsa Chica project under the supervision of Mr. Grote of Anaheim. Soon Mr. Farrell had his back wages and he, with his sisters, his team and his dogs went back to his vagabond way of life.

The natural channel of Bolsa Chica Bay, as I have said, entered into the ocean at Los Patos. The reclamation of the tideland necessitated the closing of this channel and cutting of a new one through the Mesa and hardpan just east of the Pacific electric power plant. The new cut connected Bolsa Chica Bay and Anaheim Bay.

Next, a dam with automatic tied gates had to be built, extending from a point of the Mesa south of the clubhouse to the sand dunes. This was rendered most difficult by the tremendous pressure of the title prism of water against the dam. Twice it had been washed out. I built the third dam which is still standing with its tied gates operating. The tide traveled at the rate of 3 mph. Because of the distance it had to travel, the tide coming in from Anaheim Bay through the new channel was 1 foot lower than when it came in through the old shorts channel at Los Patos. The tide gates held back the salt water when the tide was high and let out the freshwater when the tide was low, thereby keeping the salt water from going above the dam, a factor of much importance in the reclamation of the land.

In this construction work for cutting the new channel, we used fresno scrapers and road plows to start the water washing across the point of the Mesa connecting the two bays. When the water had started washing across, it was a very simple matter to plow back-and-forth and let the current carry the soil away as fast as it was loosened. I walked along the back to drive the six-horse team. At high tide only their heads and backs showed above the water. The man holding the plow was completely immersed except for his head and shoulders. When we turned the team around the ends underwater, the plow was never visible. Spectators were unable to figure it out and were curious to know what was going on, why I was driving a six-horse team back-and-forth in the water, and why a man was trailing them. I told them that I was breaking loose the hard pan so as to develop a channel to connect two bays.

We camped on the beach side and had to swim the horses across the channel in order to give them water to drink I rode one horse, tied the others to the tail of the horse ahead, and proceeded to swim them, single file, across the channel. The horse I rode was completely underwater with only his head sticking out. My head and shoulders were visible. It is hard to believe now that the channel had such depth. It is also hard to believe the difficulty we encountered in pulling the cookhouse and equipment through the soft beach sands from Huntington Beach to Bolsa Chica. Our heavy wagon was almost overtaken by the rising tide. Walter Smith, the postmaster and grocery man, found it very arduous to deliver our groceries, and on one occasion we were left two days with only a few scraps of food. This distance now requires a very few minutes on a wonderful Highway 101, but in those days it was a long, laborious trip with a team of horses in a heavily loaded wagon over the deep beach sand.

My last task was to terrace the bluff around the Bolsa Chica clubhouse. During construction a water well was drilled which showed so much gas that it cannot be used for water. The plumbers pay for the gas to the workmen's tents to be used for lighting and cooking. A large tank was later placed over the well and sealed, and natural gas was used for cooking and for letting the clubhouse for years. This was an early indication of the immense wealth of oil discovered later in the district.

Talbert's writing gives us a clear, firsthand recounting of what it was like to work the gun club project in the early 1900s. He knew the club well. But for those who never go to experience it, what was it like there day to day?

6

LIFE AT THE BOLSA CHICA GUN CLUB

I n the early 1900s, the Bolsa Chica Gun Club provided a unique opportunity for the rich and powerful members to escape the bustling cities like Los Angeles and Pasadena. The club offered a tranquil retreat where members could immerse themselves in the wild and find respite from the rigors and demands of their work life.

During this era, rapid industrialization and urbanization were transforming the landscape and lifestyle in Southern California. The cities were growing rapidly, and along with that came increased urban congestion, noise and pollution. For the affluent members of society, the gun club offered a chance to temporarily detach themselves from the pressures of city life and reconnect with nature.

Upon arriving at the Bolsa Chica Gun Club, members were greeted by the scenic beauty of the coastal wetlands and the untamed wilderness that surrounded the area. The region was teeming with diverse flora and fauna, providing a pristine environment for hunting, fishing and other recreational activities.

For many members, the gun club provided an escape from the fast-paced urban lifestyle, allowing them to reconnect with nature and engage in outdoor pursuits. They could embark on hunting expeditions across the wetlands, joining fellow club members in pursuit of waterfowl, deer and other game animals. The expansive marshes and lagoons offered a challenging and rewarding environment for those seeking adventure and the thrill of the hunt.

The Bolsa Chica Gun Club also served as a social hub, where influential individuals from different backgrounds could gather and network. Members would engage in conversations, exchange ideas and establish connections, fostering a sense of camaraderie among the elite.

The main lodging house at the Bolsa Chica Gun Club stood as a proud embodiment of the emerging architectural tradition that had gained popularity in the late 1800s—the illustrious "shingle style." This architectural movement, championed by visionaries such as Henry Hobson Richardson, sought to break away from the prevalent Gothic Revival and Victorian influences that had permeated the architectural landscape since the mid-nineteenth century. At the heart of this movement was a desire for a departure from the ornate and ostentatious in favor of a more organic, functional and harmonious design aesthetic.

As one approached the main lodging house, a sense of understated elegance prevailed. The exterior, clad in wooden shingles, presented a humble yet sophisticated façade. Unlike the flamboyantly excessive buildings of the Victorian era, this structure embraced simplicity, blending seamlessly with the natural surroundings of the Bolsa Chica Gun Club. The shingles, weathered by time, whispered stories of the coastal winds and saltwater spray, mirroring the ruggedness of the landscape.

Members pose in front of the gun club in the spring of 1904. *Author's collection.*

Stepping inside, one would be greeted by an open and spacious interior, bathed in natural light streaming through large windows. This departure from the confined and dimly lit spaces of the past was a hallmark of the shingle style. The main lodging house embraced an airy atmosphere, inviting guests to revel in the expansive views of the surrounding marshes and lagoons. These generous windows acted as portals, bridging the gap between the interior and the untamed beauty of nature that lay just beyond.

Functionality was also at the core of the shingle style, and the main lodging house at the Bolsa Chica Gun Club embodied this principle. Every detail was thoughtfully considered to enhance the experience of its inhabitants. The layout was marked by a seamless flow from one space to another, with interconnected rooms that allowed for effortless movement and social interaction. The furnishings, chosen with care, served both aesthetic and practical purposes, offering comfort and utility without sacrificing style.

The use of natural materials was yet another defining characteristic of the shingle style, and it held particular importance at the Bolsa Chica Gun Club. The interior spaces were adorned with wood elements, showcasing the beauty of the surrounding forest and reflecting a deep respect for the environment. The warm hues and rich textures of the wood imbued the lodging house with a sense of timeless charm and a connection to the natural world.

Top: Guests arriving at the Bolsa Chica Gun Club, circa 1903. *Author's collection.*

Bottom: A mother and children wait at the Red Car train stop, circa 1904. The gun club can be seen in the distance behind them. *Author's collection.*

In essence, the shingle style was not merely an architectural trend but a philosophical departure from the excesses of the past. The main lodging house at the Bolsa Chica Gun Club embraced this ethos, providing a sanctuary that blended seamlessly with its surroundings while offering open, functional spaces that celebrated natural light and the use of organic materials. In doing so, it paid homage to the legacy of the shingle style and, in turn, created an environment that encouraged harmony, tranquility and a deep appreciation for the beauty of the untamed landscape that surrounded it.

INSIDE

While limited images exist capturing the interior of the Bolsa Chica Gun Club, the few that remain offer a glimpse into a world of comfort and expansive living spaces. The rooms within exuded an air of openness, creating an atmosphere of comfort and spaciousness that welcomed its privileged guests.

The main clubhouse of the Bolsa Chica Gun Club was a remarkable architectural gem, constructed with meticulous attention to detail and a focus on creating a warm and inviting atmosphere. The building was primarily made of long, broad redwood beams, which gave it a rustic yet elegant appearance. The roofs were adorned with dark cedar shingles, adding to the overall charm of the structure.

As visitors and members entered the club, they were greeted by a plaque featuring the club's motto, "Live while you live, you'll be a long time dead." This motto served as a reminder to embrace life to the fullest, encouraging members to seize the present moment and make the most of their time at the club.

Upon entering the main room, visitors were greeted by a sight that evoked a sense of grandeur and comfort. A massive fireplace, constructed with burnt brick, stood as the centerpiece of the room. Its impressive size and craftsmanship made it a focal point, radiating a cozy ambiance throughout the space. The crackling fire would have provided warmth and a welcoming glow on cooler evenings. One notable feature was the large elk's head mounted above the central fireplace. This natural focal point added a touch of rusticity and served as a conversation starter, evoking a sense of connection with nature and the outdoors. The presence of such a majestic trophy emphasized the club's appreciation for the natural world. By embracing an earthy and simple design approach, the Bolsa Chica Gun Club's interior conveyed a sense of authenticity and understated elegance.

In addition to the main room, the clubhouse boasted a card room and a game room, both of which featured smaller fireplaces that mirrored the style of the main fireplace. These fireplaces, along with the natural

Above and opposite: Rare interior shots of the Bolsa Chica Gun Club. *Author's collection.*

materials used in the construction, contributed to a feeling of intimacy and relaxation within these recreational spaces. The earthy tones of the wood created a cozy atmosphere, enhanced by the presence of plush brown leather chairs. A poker table was a permanent fixture in this room, inviting members to engage in friendly competition, while nearby there were dominoes tables in the card room and gun room, catering to the diverse interests of the club's members.

The main recreational rooms within the clubhouse were characterized by their large and spacious interiors. The design incorporated plenty of openness, allowing natural light to flood the rooms and giving a sense of airiness. The combination of the high ceilings and the ample floor space created an environment that was both comfortable and visually appealing. The walls were adorned with various mounted fish and game trophies, showcasing the club's passion for hunting and fishing. These displays added to the rustic and traditional ambiance of the club, immersing visitors in the rich heritage and pursuits the club represented.

The Bolsa Chica Gun Club boasted a spacious and inviting dining room, characterized by its high peaked roof that gave the space an open and airy feel.

A family poses in front of the gun club in 1904. *Author's collection.*

Moving on to the residential wings of the club, each wing housed ten bedrooms. These rooms were designed to offer comfort and convenience, with double wardrobes providing ample storage space for personal belongings. Wash bowls were also included in each bedroom, ensuring that guests had access to necessary amenities. These rooms were strategically positioned to offer sweeping views of the surrounding marshland and the vast expanse of the ocean beyond. The large windows allowed guests to enjoy the breathtaking scenery and provided a serene backdrop for their stay.

Years later, as the club expanded, the structure underwent further development. Rooms were added to accommodate the growing number of members and visitors. However, the original design principles of spaciousness, natural materials and breathtaking views remained intact, ensuring that the Bolsa Chica Gun Club continued to provide a tranquil and memorable experience for all who visited.

The Bolsa Chica Gun Club not only catered to recreational activities but also provided for the practical needs of its members and staff. The clubhouse included large, well-equipped kitchens that were capable of handling the demands of a busy establishment. These kitchens were designed to facilitate the preparation of delicious meals and could accommodate multiple chefs and kitchen staff.

Adjacent to the kitchens were pantries and storage rooms. These spaces were utilized to store a wide variety of ingredients, provisions and kitchen supplies. The pantries were stocked with essential items, ensuring that the clubhouse had everything necessary to serve its guests with excellence.

One of the standout features of the Bolsa Chica Gun Club was its impressive selection of rare and fine wines. The clubhouse boasted a

The Bolsa Chica Gun Club featured a modern kitchen in the 1930s. *Huntington Library.*

The home where Bolsa Chica Gun Club founder Jaro von Schmidt resided still exists in Tustin, California. It is a designated historic landmark. *Author's collection.*

dedicated wine cellar, carefully curated to offer a diverse and coveted collection of wines from around the world. Wine enthusiasts among the club's members could indulge in the pleasure of selecting and savoring exceptional vintages.

Located at the rear of the main house was an apartment specifically designed to house gun club employees. This arrangement provided convenient accommodation for staff members, ensuring that they were readily available to attend to the needs of the club and its guests.

Surrounding the perimeter of the property were a cluster of barns and utility sheds. These structures served multiple purposes, including construction and storage. The barns provided shelter for equipment and machinery used in the maintenance and upkeep of the club's facilities. Additionally, the utility sheds offered convenient storage space for items such as tools, gardening equipment and other supplies necessary for the day-to-day operations of the club.

By incorporating these practical features into its design, the Bolsa Chica Gun Club demonstrated a commitment to providing a comprehensive experience for its members. From exquisite dining options and an extensive wine collection to comfortable employee accommodations and practical storage facilities, the clubhouse catered to the diverse needs of its community while maintaining its commitment to elegance and functionality.

Despite the club's exclusive nature as a gentlemen's retreat, the interior of the Bolsa Chica Gun Club carried the spirit of a lodge rather than that of a castle. It embraced an inviting and relaxed atmosphere, where camaraderie and shared experiences were celebrated. The rooms, while providing every comfort and luxury for its esteemed guests, avoided the grandiosity and opulence associated with castles. Instead, they exuded a sense of warmth and intimacy, inviting individuals to gather, unwind and forge lasting connections amid the untamed beauty of the surroundings.

The interplay of comfort, spaciousness and an unassuming elegance defined the interior of the Bolsa Chica Gun Club. While the limited visual records leave much to the imagination, one can envision the large, open rooms that fostered a sense of ease and relaxation. The carefully placed windows, framing the mesmerizing views, brought the outside in, allowing the natural splendor to permeate every corner. And the presence of redwood beams, mirroring the landscape, created a harmonious blend of nature and architectural design. Ultimately, the interior of the Bolsa Chica Gun Club embraced a distinct balance—where exclusivity met the welcoming embrace of a lodge and comfort coexisted with the rugged allure of the coastal retreat.

OUTSIDE

The outside grounds of the Bolsa Chica Gun Club were also truly special and exuded a captivating beauty. The main structure itself was adorned with an open veranda that encircled it, creating a charming and inviting atmosphere. The veranda featured an overhanging roof, which provided cool and comfortable shade for visitors. This architectural feature was supported by tall redwood beams, adding a touch of elegance to the surroundings.

The veranda, with its overhang and shade, offered a perfect spot for relaxation and contemplation. From this vantage point, one could gaze out at the vast expanse of the ocean, its waves crashing against the shoreline. The combination of the cool shade and the mesmerizing ocean view created a tranquil and serene environment.

Beyond the veranda lay a large, meticulously manicured grass lawn. This lawn was impeccably maintained, resembling the picturesque beauty of a British cricket field. Its lush green carpet provided a striking contrast against the blue backdrop of the sky and ocean.

To further enhance the natural beauty of the gun club, the perimeter was adorned with vibrant flowers like Easter lilies. These flowers added splashes of color and a delightful fragrance to the surroundings, creating a visually stunning display.

The outside grounds of the Bolsa Chica Gun Club were truly a sight to behold. The combination of the open veranda, well-manicured grass lawn, vibrant flowers and majestic palm trees and eucalyptus groves created a truly beautiful and captivating environment. Visitors to the gun club were greeted by a scene of natural splendor, where they could relax, enjoy the shade and take in the breathtaking views of the ocean and the surrounding landscape.

On the north side of the Bolsa Chica Gun Club's main building, adjacent to the curving drive, there was an ivy-covered arbor. This charming arbor was adorned with individually labeled rows of hooks specifically designed for hanging ducks. It served as a functional and organized space for hunters to store their harvested ducks after a successful hunting session.

Nearby, at the edge of the lagoon beneath a cliff, stood a boathouse. This boathouse was a generous gift to the club from "Uncle Lee" Borden and added to the club's amenities and infrastructure. It provided a convenient and secure location to store boats and other watercraft used by the club's members.

Tied to the dock by the boathouse were numerous small shallow boats. These boats were crucial for transporting hunters to their designated blinds within the hunting grounds. Designed to navigate shallow waters,

Top: The boats that members would take to either fish or travel to the nearby duck blinds. *Author's collection.*

Bottom: Guests on a boat traversing one of the man-made lakes at the gun club. *Author's collection.*

they were light and maneuverable, making them ideal for rowing across the lagoon. The small boats ensured that hunters could reach their blinds efficiently and quietly without disturbing the natural habitat or alerting potential prey.

The combination of the ivy-covered arbor, the boathouse and the small boats tied to the dock reflected the practical and rustic nature of the Bolsa Chica Gun Club. These elements contributed to the functionality and atmosphere of the club, providing a suitable environment for hunting activities and fostering a sense of camaraderie among its members.

THE TREES

Surrounding the establishment, a circle of eight to ten large California palms stood tall and majestic. These palm trees added a touch of grandeur to the landscape, their towering presence creating a sense of awe and wonder.

Additionally, groves of blue gum eucalyptus trees encircled the gun club, completing the picturesque scene. The blue gum eucalyptus trees, with their slender trunks and graceful branches, added a touch of elegance and natural beauty to the overall setting.

By the late 1800s, the palm tree had come to symbolize California's warm and pleasant climate. Its graceful silhouette and exotic appearance evoked images of far-off tropical destinations, such as the South Pacific. The palm tree became synonymous with leisure, relaxation and a luxurious lifestyle.

Similarly, eucalyptus trees, which were imported from Australia, also represented an idealized notion of a land of enjoyment. These tall and aromatic trees added a touch of elegance and uniqueness to the landscape. They were seen as exotic and captivating, further enhancing the allure of California as a desirable destination.

These trees played an important role in the design and selection of the flora at the Bolsa Chica Gun Club grounds. Rather than blending in with the natural surroundings, they were specifically chosen to make a statement about the idyllic climate and recreational value of the land. The intention was to create a distinct ambiance that evoked a sense of paradise and escape.

The presence of these trees, along with many of the carefully chosen flowers, helped create an artificial oasis within the untamed and chaotic swampland of the area. The gun club grounds aimed to transport visitors into a world of beauty, tranquility and leisure, contrasting with the rugged and challenging environment that lay beyond its borders.

In this sense, the landscape design of the gun club represented more of the California dream than the reality of the land. It sought to capture the essence of a perfect, year-round climate and an abundant recreational paradise. The carefully curated flora, including palm trees, eucalyptus groves and vibrant flowers, contributed to the creation of an atmosphere that was both alluring and somewhat disconnected from the natural environment.

Ultimately, the Bolsa Chica Gun Club grounds aimed to provide visitors with an escape from the ordinary and a glimpse into a Californian utopia. The carefully selected trees and flowers played a crucial role in constructing this idealized image of a land of leisure and natural beauty, even if it deviated from the true nature of the surrounding swamp land.

THE WATER SYSTEM

The Bolsa Chica Gun Club had a unique and reliable water supply system. The club sourced its water from artesian wells, providing a consistent and abundant water source for its members and facilities. The quality of the water was so exceptional that it garnered recognition and validation. An analysis of the water was conducted by Laird G. Staber, who was the esteemed head of the chemistry department at the University of Southern California (USC). The results of this analysis were proudly displayed at the entrance to the card room, showcasing the purity and excellence of the club's water supply. (Other wells would soon produce different results.)

The exceptional quality of the water was not only acknowledged but also utilized by club member Isaac Milbank. He regularly sent down ten five-gallon water bottles on the Pacific Electric train from Los Angeles to Bolsa Chica specifically to have them filled with the pristine water from the club. This further attested to the reputation and desirability of the water provided by the club's artesian wells. In the 1920s, a water tower was built on the property and can be seen looming over the main house in various photographs.

OTHER LOCAL CLUBS

Several other nearby gun clubs emerged during this period. The Westminster Club, Los Patos Gun Club, Chico Land and Water Company and numerous others were established within just several miles of the Bolsa Chica Gun Club. These clubs varied in size, with their properties ranging from ten to five thousand acres. While some of the land was utilized for farming during the appropriate seasons, other sections were used as pasturage during the dry periods of the year.

Most of these early gun clubs featured modest and unassuming wooden structures. In some cases, these structures more closely resembled farmhouses than grand lodges. Their focus was primarily on providing a functional space for club members to gather, store equipment and engage in shooting activities.

However, the Bolsa Chica Gun Club obviously went beyond the traditional model. It fully embraced the cultural trends in recreation and attitudes toward nature and wilderness that emerged during the turn of the century. The founders of the Bolsa Chica Gun Club recognized the opportunity to create a unique and impressive establishment that would stand out from the rest. As for keeping records, maps and bylaws, the club was as organized as a Fortune 500 company.

7

SHOOTING LOGS, MAPS, BYLAWS
AND MEETING NOTES

The Bolsa Chica Gun Club, known for its meticulous record-keeping, maintained comprehensive shooting logs that provided detailed information about its members' shooting activities. These logs documented various aspects of this activity, including the day of the shooting, weather conditions and specific details about each member's performance, such as the number and types of birds shot.

The shooting logs began by capturing the date of each shooting event, ensuring an accurate historical record of the club's activities over time. Weather conditions, including details like temperature, wind speed and direction, and any other relevant meteorological information that could potentially impact the shooting experience were noted. This level of detail allowed the club to analyze shooting performance in different weather conditions and make informed decisions based on the data.

Regarding individual shooting records, the logs provided precise information about each member's performance. They recorded the name of each member and documented the number of birds shot by each individual during a specific shooting session. Members were designated with unique identifiers, ensuring their privacy while maintaining accurate records.

The logs went beyond just the number of birds shot. They also documented the specific types of birds taken by each member. This information could include details such as the species of the bird, which allowed the club to monitor hunting practices and ensure adherence to hunting regulations and conservation efforts.

An original shooting log from the early 1900s. *Author's collection.*

In examining a specific shooting log from October 1, 1911, it becomes evident just how meticulously detailed the records were. The log begins with an "opening shoot" title at the top, indicating it was the start of the day's hunting activities. The weather on that particular day was noted as "cloudy," providing a glimpse into the atmospheric conditions the gun club members faced.

On the left-hand margin of the ledger, a list of a dozen gun club members is recorded, including notable individuals, such as von Schmidt and Torrance. These names represent the participants who were present for the outing, adding a personal touch to the historical account.

Running along the top of the ledger, the various bird species that were prevalent in the region at that time are meticulously listed. Species such as tufted head, mallard, pintail, cinnamon teal and green-winged teal are mentioned, among others. These details offer valuable insights into the wildlife diversity and abundance in the area during that era.

The log proceeds to highlight the individual achievements of the gun club members. On this specific outing, pintails appear to have been the most popular target among the participants. Von Schmidt successfully bagged fifteen of them, while Torrence managed to take down fourteen. Green-winged teals were also a popular choice, indicating the preferences of the hunters that day.

Furthermore, the log includes a record of the blinds used during the outing. Locations such as South Hill, Bass Lake and South Mallard are

Family members gather in front of the gun club, circa 1905. *Author's collection.*

listed, indicating the different hunting areas or positions the club members occupied during their pursuit. These details shed light on the strategies employed and the specific locations within the wetlands that were frequented by the gun club's members.

To ensure thorough documentation, the log kept a tally of the numbers harvested. This information was recorded toward the far right of the ledger, providing a clear overview of the day's achievements. Additionally, the time of return was noted, with an average ranging between 8:00 and 11:00 a.m., giving a sense of the duration of hunting trips.

The level of detail preserved in the shooting log showcases the dedication and commitment of the gun club members to keeping accurate records of their activities. It serves as a historical treasure, offering a glimpse into the practices, preferences and experiences of the Bolsa Chica Gun Club during that period.

By maintaining such meticulous shooting logs, the Bolsa Chica Gun Club demonstrated a commitment to record-keeping and data analysis, allowing them to study trends, monitor individual performance and potentially provide insights into hunting practices and bird populations. These records served as a valuable resource for the club's members and administrators, supporting their commitment to responsible hunting and environmental stewardship.

When examining a 1910 map of the Bolsa Chica Gun Club property, it becomes evident how intricately designed and expansive the club's system was for creating numerous ponds and lakes dedicated to hunting and fishing activities. The map reveals several distinct areas that were transformed

56

An early morning on the marsh, circa 1902. *Author's collection.*

and shaped by the club's efforts to seal off the ocean water inlet. These modifications were undertaken to create optimal environments for waterfowl hunting and angling.

One notable feature on the map is North Blue Lake, which was one of the prominent bodies of water within the gun club property. Its location and size suggest it served as a significant hunting and fishing spot. Another lake mentioned is Bass Lake, indicating its purpose as a habitat for bass fishing.

The map also indicates the presence of Middle Mallard Lake, Swan Lake, West Teal Lake and Goose Lake, among others. These names suggest that each body of water was tailored to accommodate specific species of waterfowl for hunting purposes. The diverse range of lakes and ponds on the property points to the club's intention to provide varied hunting experiences and attract a wide array of waterfowl species.

The map further highlights the extent of the club's landscape modifications. By sealing off the ocean water inlet, the Bolsa Chica Gun Club effectively controlled its property's water levels and created a controlled environment for hunting and fishing. This involved the construction of levees, dykes and other infrastructure to manage water flow and maintain ideal conditions for the desired species.

RULES AND BYLAWS

An 1899 copy of the Bolsa Chica Gun Club rules and bylaws provides valuable insights into the club's commitment to upholding Victorian values. Article 3 of the rules specifically emphasizes the importance of adhering to United States regulations and state game laws when engaging in shooting activities on club grounds. This articulation reflects the club's dedication to ensuring that its members participate in hunting activities in a responsible and lawful manner.

The rules also explicitly prohibit shooting on the Sabbath, indicating the club's respect for religious observances and the traditional values associated with Sundays. This prohibition aligns with Victorian ideals of moral conduct and the sanctity of the Sabbath as a day of rest and spiritual reflection.

Additionally, the document highlights the significance of opening and closing shoots, which were the main events of the year for the club. These shoots were so highly regarded and popular among the members that only the forty club members themselves were allowed to participate—no guests were permitted. This exclusivity reflects the Victorian-era emphasis on social hierarchy and the notion of membership in elite organizations.

The allocation of the most desirable blinds through a lottery system, in which lots were drawn, further reinforces the club's commitment to fairness and maintaining a sense of equity among its members. By subjecting the distribution of blinds to a random selection process, the club aimed to avoid favoritism and ensure that all members had an equal opportunity to enjoy the most sought-after shooting locations.

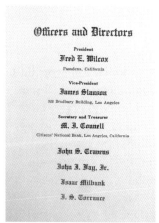

Officers and Directors

President
Fred E. Wilcox
Pasadena, California

Vice-President
James Slauson
522 Bradbury Building, Los Angeles

Secretary and Treasurer
M. J. Connell
Citizens' National Bank, Los Angeles, California

John S. Cravens

John D. Fay, Jr.

Isaac Milbank

J. S. Torrance

Top: An original copy of the club's bylaws. *Author's collection.*

Bottom: Original club bylaws. *Author's collection.*

Board Meetings

It's intriguing to see how the club was being organized even before it officially opened. The notes from the May 26, 1899 meeting, held at the California Bank building in Los Angeles, provide a glimpse into the early stages of the club's formation. Count von Schmidt's nomination as the club's first president indicates the recognition and respect he had among club members. Subsequent meetings held during that first year played a crucial role in shaping the club's structure and operations. By observing the votes taken to appoint individuals to various roles like vice-president and treasurer, we can see how the club's leadership and administrative positions were filled. It's interesting to note that the meetings were primarily held in Los Angeles, because many members had offices and business interests there. Los Angeles was a hub for the club's members, and it was where they conducted their professional activities.

The minutes from the October 15, 1936 meeting of the Bolsa Chica Gun Club also provide a fascinating glimpse into the club's activities and decision-making process. Held in the president's office, located in room 1020 in the security building on Fifth and Spring Streets in Los Angeles, the meeting commenced at 2:15 p.m.

The primary agenda for this particular meeting revolved around the election of new officers for the club. The members present deliberated on the candidates and cast their votes to determine the club's leadership for the upcoming term. This process involved discussions regarding the qualifications and suitability of each candidate.

Apart from the election, the minutes also documented meticulous budget discussions and decisions. The club's financial matters, including income, expenditures and proposed investments, were thoroughly reviewed and deliberated during the meeting. These budget conversations played a crucial role in shaping the club's financial stability and planning for future endeavors.

Interestingly, among the various club business matters discussed, there was a noteworthy decision regarding Marjorie C. Welch. Marjorie, being the niece of the late Michael J. Connell, was reported to have a deep affection for the club. Since Connell did not leave a widow, the members present at the meeting elected Marjorie as a member of the Bolsa Chica Gun Club. This decision recognized Marjorie's connection to the club through her late uncle and her own demonstrated interest in maintaining his legacy within the organization.

Family members posing in front of the club in March 1905. *Author's collection.*

These detailed minutes offer a valuable historical record, shedding light on the inner workings of the Bolsa Chica Gun Club during that particular meeting in 1936. They provide a glimpse into the club's governance and decision-making processes and the individuals involved in shaping its direction and membership. Thankfully, records of many meeting minutes still exist. But what about the actual members? Who were they? What did they do? What about the guests and workers? Let's look at who you would have actually seen at the Bolsa Chica Gun Club.

8

MEMBERS, GUESTS AND WORKERS

On any given day at the Bolsa Chica Gun Club, one would encounter a vibrant tapestry of individuals representing diverse backgrounds and roles within the establishment. The club attracted an assortment of well-to-do and prominent people, ranging from successful business executives to influential community leaders. Among them, notable guests would frequently grace the club's premises, including celebrities, politicians and accomplished athletes. However, the heart of the club's operations lay in its dedicated workforce, who tirelessly ensured the smooth functioning of the facility. These workers, including maintenance staff and administrative personnel, formed the backbone of the club, diligently catering to the needs of members and guests alike. Together, this eclectic mix of people created a unique atmosphere that fostered camaraderie, provided a platform for networking and celebrated a shared passion for shooting sports.

PROMINENT MEMBERS

Hulett C. Merritt, a prominent early member of the Bolsa Chica Gun Club, was a well-known figure in Los Angeles during the early twentieth century. Described as a "millionaire and financier" by the *Los Angeles Herald* in 1910, Merritt was actively involved in both business and civic affairs.

Merritt gained attention in 1910 due to his plans to construct the Merritt building in downtown Los Angeles. He lobbied the city council to remove the height restrictions on buildings, which, at the time, limited a building's height to between 180 and 233 feet. Merritt argued that the height restriction would compromise the architectural beauty of his proposed building. He emphasized that his main motivation was to create a structure of artistic value rather than pursue financial gain. This demonstrates his appreciation for aesthetics and his commitment to contributing to the city's architectural landscape.

Originally from Minnesota, Merritt had a successful career as a businessman. In 1891, he sold his shares in the Merritt-Rockefeller syndicate for a staggering amount of over $81 million. This significant financial achievement further solidified his status as a wealthy individual.

Another notable member of the Bolsa Chica Gun Club was James Slauson. Slauson, a prominent land developer in nineteenth-century Southern California, played a key role in the establishment of the town of Azusa and also served as the mayor of Austin, Nevada. Slauson acquired approximately 5,800 acres of land situated to the east of Los Angeles, earning him the titles "the father of citrus fruit culture in the foothill region" and "the father of the town of Azusa." In 1886, he sold half of this land to J.D. Bicknell, I.W. Hellman and others, while retaining 800 acres for himself, which he then incorporated as the Azusa Land and Water Company. Subsequently, he laid out the town's design and planted high-quality "orange and lemon trees" in the area. Additionally, Slauson expanded his land ownership to include properties in Ontario, California, and Los Angeles.

As president of the Los Angeles Chamber of Commerce and the Sunset Club, a prominent social organization, Slauson made significant contributions to the establishment and support of churches throughout Southern California. In addition to his involvement in the business and social spheres, Slauson was known for his philanthropy. He supported various charitable causes, including the Boys' Home at Garvanza, the Los Angeles YMCA, a Los Angeles orphan asylum and the Salvation Army Rescue Home. Furthermore, he played a key role in raising funds for the construction of a monument dedicated to Spanish-American War veterans in Central Park, which is now known as Pershing Square. Slauson's philanthropic efforts left a lasting impact on the community and reflected his commitment to the welfare and betterment of Southern California.

In Los Angeles, there is a road named Slauson Avenue, which is named after James Slauson. Slauson Avenue runs east-west through several neighborhoods in Los Angeles, including South Los Angeles, Florence and Downey. It spans approximately seventeen miles, starting at the Los Angeles

River in the west and extending to the city of Whittier in the east. The road was named in honor of Slauson's contributions to the development and progress of the city of Los Angeles. It serves as a reminder of his legacy and impact on the local community.

Hampton L. Story, a member of the Bolsa Chica Gun Club, was a prominent figure with diverse professional and civic engagements. He held significant positions in various industries and organizations, demonstrating his influence and involvement in multiple fields.

Story and Clark was a prominent piano and organ company that was established by Hampton L. Story in in Chicago in 1888. He opened his first music store in Burlington, Vermont, in 1859. In 1862, Story entered a partnership with a piano builder named Powers, and together they formed the Story and Powers Company. This collaboration marked the birth of the first piano manufacturing company in Vermont. It focused on producing high-quality pianos and gained a reputation for its craftsmanship and attention to detail.

Outside of his professional engagements, Story was also a member of the Pasadena Audubon Society, demonstrating his interest in birdwatching, conservation, and the natural world. This affiliation suggests that he was environmentally conscious and participated in activities and initiatives related to preserving and appreciating nature.

Also, Story was the founder of the iconic Hotel del Coronado, a luxurious beachfront hotel located in Coronado, California. The hotel, known for its grand Victorian architecture, has been a landmark and popular destination for over a century. Story's role as its founder highlights his entrepreneurial spirit and vision in establishing a renowned hospitality establishment.

Hampton's proficiency with keyboards was unparalleled. His mastery of various musical genres, including classical, jazz and contemporary, allowed him to create enchanting organ programs that would transport listeners to new realms of musical bliss. His performances at the gun club were eagerly anticipated by members, who found solace and joy in the harmonious melodies that emanated from his skilled hands. With each stroke of the keys, Hampton effortlessly breathed life into the organ, transforming it into an instrument of pure magic. His fingers danced across the keyboard, navigating intricate melodies and harmonies with ease. The gun club's hall would fill with the rich, resonant sounds, enveloping everyone in a symphony of emotions.

Hampton's performances were not limited to the traditional organ repertoire. He would often infuse his programs with innovative arrangements and improvisations, injecting his own unique style into every piece. This creative approach added an element of surprise and excitement, leaving the audience in awe of his technical prowess and imaginative interpretations.

The gun club members were impressed by not only Hampton's musicianship but also his keen understanding of keyboard manufacturing. He would often share his knowledge and insights, discussing the intricacies of different keyboard mechanisms and the evolution of musical instruments over time. His passion for the craft was contagious, and his conversations sparked lively debates and inspired fellow members to explore their own musical interests. Hampton's performances at the gun club were transformative experiences for all who had the pleasure of listening. His keyboard playing talents brought people together, fostering a sense of community and camaraderie among the members. It was during these moments that the gun club transcended its conventional purpose and became a sanctuary of musical appreciation.

Gail B. Johnson was another original member of the Bolsa Chica Gun Club. He held various positions of influence, including as a director of the German American Savings Bank (later First National Bank) and vice-president of Pacific Mutual Life Insurance Company. Johnson was also a board member of the Los Angeles Chamber of Commerce, indicating his involvement in the business community and his interest in promoting economic development in the region.

Isaac Milbank, another member of the club, was a prosperous businessman in Los Angeles. Co-founder of the Borden Milk Company, Milbank was also an oil investor and the holder of several firearms patents as well as an active participant in local business and social affairs.

J.D. Thomson, hailing from Pasadena, was a member of the Bolsa Chica Gun Club as well. He had connections to various oil and mining companies, including the Premier and Mascot Oil Companies, the Hidalgo Oil Company and the Boca del Cobre and Sierra Pinta mining companies. Thomson's affiliations with these companies suggest his involvement in the extractive industries, particularly oil and mining, which were significant economic sectors in California at the time.

William Bayly had connections to H.E. Huntington, an influential figure involved in the creation of Naples for the West Coast. Bayly collaborated with Huntington in the development and planning of the Naples community, which was intended to be a resort area in California. His association with Huntington suggests his involvement in real estate and development projects.

Moses Sherman was a prominent figure in the development and growth of Southern California, particularly the San Fernando Valley area. Sherman

Moses Sherman. *Author's collection.*

Oaks, a neighborhood in Los Angeles, was named after him, highlighting his significant contributions to the region. In 1927, Sherman purchased one thousand acres of land in the area that is now known as Sherman Oaks. He embarked on a development project, transforming the land into a residential neighborhood. Sherman's vision for Sherman Oaks was to create a suburban enclave that offered a peaceful and family-friendly lifestyle while maintaining convenient access to Los Angeles. One of Sherman's other notable achievements was his role in bringing the streetcar system to the San Fernando Valley. Upon arriving in Los Angeles in 1890, Sherman, who had previously established a street railway in Phoenix, set out to revolutionize the local transportation system. In a city where predominantly horse-drawn cars operated on small street railways, Sherman embarked on a mission to consolidate and electrify these fragmented networks. His efforts resulted in the formation of the Los Angeles Consolidated Electric Railway, marking the inception of the city's first electrified street railway. Through strategic acquisitions, Sherman expanded and interconnected the rail lines, establishing an extensive and modernized transportation network in the heart of Los Angeles.

Today, Sherman's impact on Southern California is still evident. The San Fernando Valley, which he recognized as a promising area for development, has grown into one of the largest and most populous regions in the country. The road "Sherman Way" is named for him and "Hazeltine Avenue" in Sherman Oaks is named for his daughter.

John McWilliams Jr. was a conservative businessman originally from Illinois who managed real estate holdings in the Pasadena and Los Angeles region. He met his first wife, Julia, in Chicago in 1903, and they married in 1911. Shortly after their marriage, they relocated to Pasadena, where John took over his father's land management business.

In 1912, the couple welcomed a daughter named Julia, who would eventually become famous as a chef, American television personality and writer known as Julia Child. She played a significant role in making French cuisine accessible to American audiences and gained widespread recognition for her culinary expertise. John McWilliams himself was a very active member of the club, and there are a few stories that have been passed down

Above: A young child poses in front of the Bolsa Chica Gun Club, circa 1905. *Author's collection.*

Left: Jared Torrance. *Author's collection.*

over the years about him bringing his young daughter to the club around 1920. These visits would occur on the days when women and children were allowed to visit the club. Julia's visits provided her an opportunity to experience the club's atmosphere and activities firsthand.

Jared Sidney Torrance was a prominent real estate developer and the founder of the city of Torrance in California. Born in New York in 1852, Torrance relocated to California in the 1880s. His visionary efforts and innovative approach to urban planning left a lasting impact on the development of the city that bears his name. In 1912, while a member of the Bolsa Chica Gun Club, Torrance founded the city of Torrance on land he had acquired in the South Bay region of Los Angeles County. His goal was to create a model industrial community with a diverse economy that would attract both businesses and residents. Torrance envisioned a city that would provide a high-quality living environment for its inhabitants.

One of Torrance's notable contributions was his emphasis on urban planning and design. He carefully crafted the layout of the city, incorporating wide streets, spacious parks and a gridiron street pattern that allowed for easy navigation and accessibility to all parts of the city. This thoughtful design promoted a sense of openness and provided residents with well-planned public spaces to enjoy. He had also embarked on a mission to establish a "workingman's paradise," envisioning a pioneering residential and industrial city located midway between Los Angeles and the San Pedro Harbor. Torrance successfully enticed prominent industrial companies and a railroad to move their operations to this new city. Renowned landscape architects Olmsted and Olmsted, with additional contributions from modernist architect Irving J. Gill and landscape architect Frank Lloyd Wright Jr. collaborated to craft the city's unique aesthetic. The resulting architectural style, a fusion of Mission Revival and early Modernist influences, showcased distinctive features such as the iconic depot and railroad bridge.

Additionally, Torrance established the Torrance School District, which became renowned for its commitment to delivering high-quality education to its students. This dedication to education helped foster a strong sense of community and contributed to the overall appeal of Torrance as a desirable place to live and raise a family. Through Torrance's efforts, the city thrived and grew into a vibrant community. In 1920, Torrance established the Torrance Hospital Association, with the intention of building a hospital in the newly established city. Regrettably, Jared passed away before seeing his vision come to fruition. However, his widow, Helena Childs Torrance, carried on his legacy, and in 1925, the Jared Sidney Torrance Memorial Hospital was successfully opened. Today, it is known as the Torrance Memorial Medical Center, a testament to the enduring impact of the Torrance family's commitment to healthcare in the community.

H. Lee Borden was the son of Gail Borden Jr., the inventor of condensed milk and founder of the Borden Dairy Company in 1857. Born into a prominent family, H. Lee Borden carried on his father's legacy and made contributions of his own. Apart from his involvement in the Borden Dairy business, H. Lee Borden was also a member of the Bolsa Chica Gun Club. Borden had a keen interest in hunting and was an active participant in the club's activities. In fact, Borden played a significant role in the development of the club. He financed the construction of the boathouse, as well as the acquisition of forty hunting boats that were used by club members. His contributions helped establish the club as a popular destination for hunting enthusiasts. Tragically, H. Lee Borden's life came to an untimely end in November 1902. It was reported that he died in a Los Angeles hotel after consuming a duck (at the Bolsa Chica Gun Club a couple of days earlier) that had allegedly been improperly stored, leading to ptomaine poisoning. Interestingly, there were no repercussions for the club, and the story remains essentially a forgotten footnote.

On August 19, 1935, the city of Los Angeles mourned the loss of another prominent figure, Michael J. Connell. The Bolsa Chica Gun Club member was known for his accomplishments as a banker, civil leader and philanthropist. Connell's passing sent shockwaves through the community. Michael J. Connell was a man of great influence and wealth, having established himself as one of the city's most respected individuals. He had dedicated his life to the pursuit of financial success and had become renowned for his astute business acumen. Born into a humble family, Connell's rise to prominence was a testament to his unwavering determination and hard work. Over the years, his reputation as a shrewd banker grew, and he amassed considerable wealth through his various business ventures. With his financial success, Connell became deeply committed to giving back to the community that had supported him. As a civil leader, Connell took an active role in local politics and had a deep passion for social causes. He believed in the power of education and spearheaded numerous initiatives to improve access to quality schooling for underprivileged children. Connell's philanthropic endeavors extended to healthcare, where he generously funded medical research and established clinics to provide care for those in need.

Connell's impact on the city of Los Angeles was far-reaching. His contributions transcended financial support, as he actively participated in

A gun club member, possibly H. Lee Borden, near the boat launch in 1902. *Author's collection.*

community events and championed various initiatives that aimed to uplift and empower the less fortunate. His dedication and selflessness earned him the respect and admiration of his peers and the general public alike.

Tragically, it was at the Bolsa Chica Gun Club that Connell's life was unexpectedly cut short. While engaging in his recreational pursuits, he suffered a sudden heart attack, which he died from several days later. The news of his passing reverberated throughout the city, leaving a void that was not easily filled. The loss of Michael J. Connell was deeply felt by all those who had been touched by his kindness, generosity and leadership. In the wake of his untimely death, the legacy of Michael J. Connell lived on. His name would forever be associated with the positive changes he brought to the community and the lives he touched. The residence he had built for himself and his family on South Figueroa Street would stand as a testament to his achievements and the enduring impact he had on Los Angeles.

A SPECIAL GUEST

George von Lengerke Meyer was a regular visitor to the club starting in about 1910, when he became the United States' Secretary of the Navy. Meyer was an American businessman, politician and diplomat who served in various high-ranking positions during the late nineteenth and early twentieth centuries. He was born on June 24, 1858, in Boston, Massachusetts, and passed away on March 9, 1918.

Meyer began his career in the business world, working in his family's shipping business. He gained valuable experience and eventually became involved in other industries, including banking and finance. His success in business and his reputation as a skilled negotiator and diplomat led to his entry into politics. He was speaker of the Massachusetts House of Representatives from 1894 to 1896. In 1901, President William McKinley appointed Meyer as the United States ambassador to Italy, a position he held until 1905. He then served as the ambassador to Russia from 1905 to 1907 under President Theodore Roosevelt. Meyer's diplomatic skills and international experience made him a valuable asset in maintaining and strengthening relationships between the United States and these countries. He was then appointed as the postmaster general under Roosevelt from 1907 to 1909. As postmaster general, Meyer implemented various reforms to improve the efficiency and effectiveness of the postal service.

In 1909, Roosevelt appointed Meyer Secretary of the Navy. During his tenure, Meyer focused on modernizing and expanding the U.S. Navy, advocating for a strong naval presence and the development of new ships. He also played a significant role in improving naval policies and relations with other countries.

After leaving the position of Secretary of the Navy in 1913, Meyer retired from public service and returned to his business interests. He continued to be involved in various philanthropic activities and held leadership positions in several organizations. Whenever he visited the gun club, he supposedly demonstrated an extremely keen eye for shooting. The press loved covering his visits.

Meyer had a special affinity for Bass Lake, one of the prized shooting stations on the club's property. The serene beauty and challenging shooting opportunities offered by Bass Lake made it a favorite among many members, including Secretary Meyer. He would frequently be taken to this location to partake in the exhilarating sport of shooting.

Given the prestige associated with Secretary Meyer's position and the respect he commanded, it was only natural that members of the Bolsa Chica

George von Lengerke Meyer.
Author's collection.

Gun Club would eagerly vie for the opportunity to be included in his shooting team. Being part of his team not only brought a sense of honor and recognition but also provided an avenue for networking and camaraderie among the club members.

Securing a spot on Secretary Meyer's team required not only skill and proficiency in shooting but also a strong commitment to the values and camaraderie fostered by the gun club. Members who were fortunate enough to be included in his team would gain invaluable insights and guidance from Secretary Meyer himself, further honing their shooting abilities and deepening their understanding of the sport.

The inclusion of Secretary Meyer in shooting activities at Bass Lake added an extra layer of excitement and prestige to the experience for club members. His presence elevated the atmosphere and served as a testament to the club's commitment to excellence and its close ties with influential individuals. The opportunity to interact with and shoot alongside Secretary Meyer provided members with unique networking prospects. It facilitated connections and relationships that extended beyond the gun club, potentially opening doors to professional opportunities and furthering their passion for the sport.

A family poses in front of the Bolsa Chica Gun Club in the early 1900s. *Author's collection.*

Secretary Meyer's regular visits to Bass Lake and the accompanying camaraderie and prestige associated with his shooting team further solidified the Bolsa Chica Gun Club's reputation as a distinguished and revered institution among shooting enthusiasts.

DID THEODORE ROOSEVELT EVER VISIT?

It is a common misconception (that has been widely documented) that President Theodore Roosevelt visited the Bolsa Chica Gun Club during his first trip to California in 1903. While it is easy to imagine that he may have visited, given his love of hunting, there is no historical evidence to support this claim. A comprehensive timeline of Roosevelt's activities during his stay in the Los Angeles area reveals a tightly woven tapestry of commitments, leaving no room for leisurely visits or spontaneous detours.

DID BABE RUTH AND LOU GEHRIG VISIT THE BOLSA CHICA GUN CLUB?

A photograph of Babe Ruth and Lou Gehrig hunting at a gun club, taken in October 1927, is an iconic image in baseball history, and it has been widely circulated and reproduced in various forms over the years. The photograph has been mislabeled as having been taken at the Bolsa Chica Gun Club, but it was not. The photograph was actually taken at the Farmers Gun Club in nearby Los Alamitos, confirmed by the family of Glenn Thomas, the man in the photograph with the ballplayers.

Left to right: Lou Gehrig, Glenn Thomas and Babe Ruth in 1927. This photograph was taken at the Farmers Gun Club, which was located near Bolsa Chica in Los Alamitos. *Author's collection.*

THE OKUDAS

In 2006, esteemed author/professor David Carlberg had the opportunity to interview Jim Okuda, a fascinating individual with a unique connection to history. From 1910 to 1935, Jim's father served as the groundskeeper at the Bolsa Chica Gun Club, and it was during those years that Jim's childhood unfolded in the beautiful coastal town of Huntington Beach.

Born in 1921, Jim grew up alongside his parents and siblings in a house nestled below the grand clubhouse. When Jim wasn't attending school locally, his days were filled with the simple joys of fishing and swimming in the nearby lagoon. He would also lend a hand in tending to his mother's chickens and relished the breathtaking sunsets from the nearby beach.

However, amid the idyllic backdrop of his upbringing, Jim's life took an unexpected turn. As he helped his father care for the lush landscaping surrounding the clubhouse, he had the opportunity to witness a procession of luxury cars, chauffeured by a fleet of polished drivers. These vehicles would deposit an array of notable guests, including bankers, industry leaders, sports figures and even Hollywood stars.

Among the visitors who caught young Jim's attention was a slim, unassuming gentleman who quietly made his way into the clubhouse—an encounter that would later be revealed to him as a meeting with none other than the prince of Wales. This unassuming visitor would, in a mere two years, ascend to the throne as King Edward VIII of Great Britain.

Jim's memory of that encounter with the future king was etched into his mind, forever capturing the grandeur and significance of the moment. It was a remarkable glimpse into a world far beyond the reach of his humble abode, where he had the chance to witness history in the making.

As the years passed, Jim Okuda's life would take its own course, but the memories of his childhood at the Bolsa Chica Gun Club and the extraordinary encounters there would remain with him, serving as a testament to the captivating and unpredictable nature of life's journey. In addition to the grandeur of the clubhouse and the occasional encounters with notable guests, duck hunting was a major activity that enthralled Jim during his time at the club. Each morning, avid hunters were transported to the expansive freshwater ponds that stretched across much of the Bolsa Chica property.

The Bolsa Chica Gun Club in the early 1930s. Note the pristine front lawn. *Huntington Library.*

Jim vividly recalled the anticipation and excitement that filled the air as the hunters prepared for their day in the marshes. Instead of relying on trained dogs to retrieve downed ducks, the club had a unique system in place. Local boys, donning hip boots, were hired to carry out this essential task. Although Jim was not yet old enough to participate as a "bird dog," he eagerly tagged along, captivated by the sights and sounds that unfolded before him.

As the hunters took their positions, the tranquility of the marshland would be broken by the unmistakable crack of gunfire. The sudden eruption of sound would startle the thousands of ducks that called the Bolsa Chica home. In an awe-inspiring spectacle, the sky would transform as the startled ducks took flight, their wings creating a symphony of beating feathers.

For Jim, the sight was nothing short of breathtaking. The sheer number of waterfowl ascending into the sky, their wings whirring in unison, left an indelible mark on his memory. It was a moment of pure natural wonder, as if the very essence of the Bolsa Chica came alive in that instant. The cacophony of quacks and the beating of wings reverberated in his ears, a testament to the power and beauty of the avian world.

While Jim couldn't yet join the ranks of the hunters or the hired boys retrieving the ducks, he absorbed every detail of the experience. The camaraderie, the thrill of the hunt and the breathtaking display of nature's majesty all left an enduring impression on his young mind. It was an education in the rhythms of life, the delicate balance between man and nature and the timeless traditions that unfolded in those early morning hours.

As the years passed, Jim would carry these memories with him, cherishing the moments spent on the Bolsa Chica, where the echoes of gunshots mingled with the symphony of wings, forever etching the beauty of the marshland and the joy of duck hunting into his soul.

March 10, 1933, was a night that forever etched itself into Jim's memory. As twilight settled over the coastal town, an unimaginable force rippled through the earth, shaking the very foundations of the land. The powerful 6.4 magnitude earthquake, now known as the "Long Beach earthquake," had arrived, its origins traced back to the movement of the Inglewood/Newport Fault.

The gun club, primarily constructed of wood, was fortunate in its resilience to the tempestuous tremors. Despite the violent shaking, the club's buildings withstood the onslaught relatively well.

However, the same could not be said for the road leading up to the clubhouse and the dam that held the surrounding waters at bay. As the earth convulsed, deep cracks tore through the once solid ground. The road, once

Inspectors survey the damage after the March 19, 1933 Long Beach earthquake. The Bolsa Chica Gun Club can be seen in the background. *Author's collection.*

A similar view today. *Photograph by Tamara Asaki.*

a smooth path for visitors and members alike, now resembled a fragmented puzzle, its pieces scattered and displaced by the immense power unleashed by nature. Jim vividly remembered surveying the aftermath in the wake of the earthquake. The road he had traversed countless times, a familiar route that led to the heart of the club, was now a treacherous obstacle course of jagged crevices. The dam, a symbol of stability and order, had not escaped unscathed either, as deep cracks marred its once unyielding façade. The scene was a testament to the raw power of nature, a reminder that even amid tranquility, the very ground beneath their feet could be transformed into a force of chaos. It was a humbling experience for Jim, a stark reminder of the fragility of human structures in the face of nature's might.

In the aftermath of the earthquake, efforts were made to repair the damage and restore normalcy. The cracks on the road were filled, and the dam underwent meticulous repairs. The resilience of the gun club's wooden buildings served as a testament to the craftsmanship of their construction.

The memory of that fateful evening stayed with Jim throughout his life. It became a vivid reminder of the unpredictable nature of existence, a chapter in the story of the Bolsa Chica and its enduring connection to the forces that shape the world. It served as a reminder to cherish the moments of tranquility and appreciate the strength and resilience that emerges in the face of adversity.

The Okuda family's tenure at the Bolsa Chica Gun Club was marked by hard work, dedication and a strong sense of community. Led by Harry Okuda, the Japanese American family played an integral role in maintaining the club's landscaping and kitchen gardens, as well as tending to various other responsibilities that contributed to the smooth functioning of the club.

Living in a house situated below the clubhouse, the Okuda family experienced a unique blend of work and home life. Their proximity to the heart of the gun club allowed them to immerse themselves fully in the day-to-day operations of the club and build close relationships with club members and staff.

Harry Okuda, as the head of the family, took charge of managing the club's landscaping. With a meticulous eye for detail, he ensured that the grounds surrounding the clubhouse were beautifully maintained. This included maintaining the yard of chickens, which provided fresh eggs for club member dinners, adding a touch of self-sufficiency and farm-to-table quality to the club's dining experience.

The Okuda children played an active role in assisting their father with his work. They eagerly accompanied him as he cared for the landscaping, and their small hands helped tend to the plants, flowers and trees that adorned the club's premises. Their involvement created a sense of unity within the family, as they worked together to contribute to the club's aesthetic appeal.

One notable responsibility the Okuda family undertook was the care of a nine-hole golf course located on the gun club's grounds. Maintaining the course involved tasks such as mowing the grass, ensuring the fairways were well-groomed and maintaining the overall integrity of the golfing experience for club members. This role enabled Harry Okuda and his children to witness the joy and camaraderie that golf brought to the club, fostering a deep appreciation for the sport.

Living and working at the Bolsa Chica gun club, the Okuda family became an integral part of the club's extended family. They formed lasting friendships with club members and were respected for their hard work and dedication. Their presence created a sense of continuity and stability, as they diligently carried out their responsibilities year after year. While the Okuda family's time at the gun club coincided with a period of racial and social challenges for Japanese Americans, their contributions were recognized and valued within the club community. Their work ethic and commitment to the club's success transcended any barriers, and they left a lasting legacy in the memories of those who had the privilege of knowing and working alongside them.

The Okuda family's experience at the Bolsa Chica Gun Club was one of dedication, community and shared responsibility. Through their tireless efforts in maintaining the club's landscaping and kitchen gardens, as well as caring for the golf course, they contributed to the club's atmosphere of beauty and hospitality. Their presence enriched the lives of club members and left an enduring impression on the history of the Bolsa Chica Gun Club.

The Okuda family, much like many of Orange County's Japanese Americans, found themselves uprooted from their California home when World War II broke out. The Okudas, along with countless other Japanese Americans, were forcibly uprooted from their homes, forced to leave behind familiar landscapes and embark on a journey to the Colorado River Relocation Center in Poston, Arizona. It was a time of immense struggle and uncertainty, as they faced the challenges of living within the confines of an internment camp. Yet despite the hardships, the Okuda family, like many others, found strength within their community. They supported each other, held onto their hopes and persevered through the darkest of times. Their story, like the stories of countless Japanese Americans during that era, serves as a reminder of the resilience and spirit that can emerge even in the face of adversity.

Tragedy at the Gun Club

It was a crisp autumn day in 1915 when a Japanese man named Kamino Senzo met his untimely demise. Senzo was known to be a hardworking employee at the gun club, responsible for hauling alfalfa. On that fateful day, he found himself on top of a wagon loaded with alfalfa bales, making his way across a bridge. The wheels of the wagon wobbled, causing the load to shift. In a desperate attempt to regain balance, Senzo was thrown forward and tragically tumbled off the wagon. Before anyone could react, the wheels rolled over his head, causing instant and fatal injuries.

The news of the accident quickly reached the ears of Mr. Andrews, the superintendent of the gun club. Deeply saddened by the loss, he promptly contacted the coroner's office to report the incident. The lifeless body of Kamino Senzo was carefully transported to his home, approximately two miles away from the club. His residence was part of a vibrant enclave called Wintersburg, predominantly populated by Japanese American farmers. Wintersburg was a close-knit community, where families worked the land, cultivating crops and nurturing their dreams. The loss of Kamino Senzo shook the community to its core. They mourned the passing of a hardworking man, whose dedication and diligence were widely admired.

Memories from J.A. Graves

In his 1928 book, *My 70 Years in California*, J.A. Graves provides a description of a standard outing to the Bolsa Chica Gun Club. According to Graves, in 1911, the preferred mode of transportation to the gun club was either taking the Pacific Electric Red Car or hitching a ride in a friend's automobile, which was commonly referred to as a "machine" during that time.

Choosing to travel by automobile had its advantages, as it allowed the club members to avoid a dark and somewhat arduous two-mile journey from the Pacific Electric stop to the club in a mule-pulled wagon. However, it also meant sharing the unpaved roads with slow wagons hauling sugar beets, which could slow down the journey.

Once the club members arrived at the gun club, they would meet with other members who were planning to go shooting the following day. They would enjoy hearty dinners together, and after dinner, they would spend the evening engaged in activities such as chatting, reading, playing card games and simply relaxing.

Members arrived at
the gun club in 1904.
Author's collection.

The keeper of the gun club would awaken the members early the next day, typically at 5:00 a.m., by rapping on their doors. The members would then proceed to put on their hunting gear, have breakfast and head out into the darkness toward the blinds. It was customary for shooting to commence approximately thirty minutes before sunrise, which was signaled by the ringing of a bell. This bell served as a notification to all club members that they were now permitted to start shooting.

Graves's description portrays a typical outing to the Bolsa Chica Gun Club in the early twentieth century, highlighting the transportation methods, camaraderie among members and the daily routines associated with hunting and shooting activities.

HENRY HUNTINGTON

Of all the Bolsa Chica Gun Club's prominent members, Henry Huntington is arguably the most notable. After all, it was during his time spent at the club that it is believed he first heard about Pacific City, a small establishment just a few miles down the coast, which he would purchase in 1903, thus creating the city of Huntington Beach. Henry Huntington, born on February 27, 1850, in Oneonta, New York, was a remarkable individual whose contributions to transportation and philanthropy left an indelible mark on American society. Known for his entrepreneurial spirit, shrewd business acumen and philanthropic endeavors, Huntington's legacy continues to inspire generations.

Huntington's early life was marked by a deep curiosity and thirst for knowledge. He was the nephew of Collis P. Huntington, one of the "Big Four" businessmen involved in the construction of the Central Pacific Railroad. Under his uncle's guidance, Huntington gained invaluable insights into the world of transportation and business at a young age. These formative experiences would shape his future endeavors.

After working for several railroad companies, in 1892, Henry Huntington moved to San Francisco to join his uncle, who was president of the Southern Pacific Company. During a period of booming Southern California land development, Huntington acquired the city-focused Los Angeles Railway (LARy), also known as the "Yellow Car" system, in 1898 in a friendly rivalry with his uncle's Southern Pacific. Subsequently, in 1901, he established the expansive standard gauge Pacific Electric Railway (PE), dubbed the "Red Car" system, with its hub located at Sixth and Main Streets in Los Angeles. Huntington outperformed his competitors by offering passenger-friendly streetcars operating on 24/7 schedules, a service level unmatched by the railroads. This venture was a resounding success and transformed the city's transportation landscape.

Huntington's impact on transportation extended far beyond Los Angeles. The development of the extensive Pacific Electric Railway connected Los Angeles with many neighboring cities and suburbs. The "Red Cars," as they came to be known, facilitated the growth of Southern California and played a vital role in shaping the region's urbanization.

Beyond his accomplishments in transportation, Huntington's philanthropic efforts were equally significant. Inspired by his passion for collecting rare books and artwork, he established the Huntington Library, Art Gallery and Botanical Gardens in San Marino, California. The institution, opened to the public in 1928, houses a vast collection of rare books, manuscripts and artwork, including the Gutenberg Bible and Thomas Gainsborough's famous painting *The Blue Boy*.

Huntington's philanthropic endeavors were not limited to the arts. He also made significant contributions to education and research. He played

Henry Huntington. *Author's collection.*

an instrumental role in the growth of the California Institute of Technology (Caltech) and provided generous support for the institution throughout his life. His vision and financial backing helped shape Caltech into one of the world's leading scientific and technological institutions.

Henry Huntington's contributions to transportation and philanthropy continue to impact society today. The streetcar systems he established laid the foundation for modern mass transit systems, and his philanthropic institutions serve as beacons of knowledge and culture.

Huntington passed away on May 23, 1927, leaving behind a lasting legacy that transcends his lifetime. His entrepreneurial spirit, vision and commitment to improving society through transportation and philanthropy serve as an enduring inspiration for future generations. His ability to recognize opportunities, navigate complex business landscapes and combine his passion for art and education with his entrepreneurial pursuits set him apart as a true visionary. But in terms of the story of the Bolsa Chica Gun Club, Huntington's introduction of the local electric railway system was truly a game changer.

9

THE BIRTH OF HUNTINGTON BEACH AND THE RED CARS THAT ARRIVED

The membership of Henry Huntington in the Bolsa Chica Gun Club holds great historic timing and significance, as it played a pivotal role in the birth of what is now known as Huntington Beach. It was during his time as a member of this club that Huntington discovered a small enclave called Pacific City a few miles down the coast; this would shape the course of his future endeavors.

In the early 1900s, Huntington was an influential businessman and entrepreneur with a keen interest in real estate and transportation. As he heard about Pacific City (often while at the gun club), he recognized the potential for development and growth in the area. With the guidance of his team of advisors, he made the decision to purchase Pacific City, setting in motion a series of events that would transform the coastal community into the vibrant city it is today.

The acquisition of Pacific City by Huntington and his team marked the beginning of a deliberate and strategic effort to develop the area into a thriving beachside destination. They focused on creating a unique and attractive environment that would draw visitors and residents alike. This vision included the construction of a pier, the establishment of hotels and residential areas and the promotion of recreational activities such as surfing and beach culture. Under Huntington's leadership and influence, Pacific City underwent significant transformation and development. It was renamed Huntington Beach in 1903 (and incorporated in 1909) in honor of its visionary founder. The city quickly gained a reputation as a popular seaside resort and a hub for beach-related activities.

Huntington's foresight and entrepreneurial spirit greatly impacted the growth and character of Huntington Beach. His investment and commitment to the area laid the foundation for its future as a vibrant coastal city known for its beautiful beaches, vibrant surfing culture and thriving tourism industry. Today, Huntington Beach is recognized as one of Southern California's premier coastal destinations, attracting millions of visitors each year and serving as a cherished home for residents.

The historic timing of Huntington's membership in the Bolsa Chica Gun Club and his subsequent discovery and acquisition of Pacific City cannot be overstated. It was through this sequence of events that the vision, resources and determination of Henry Huntington came together to shape the birth of Huntington Beach, leaving a lasting impact on the region and establishing a legacy that continues to thrive to this day.

The *Los Angeles Times* report from May 19, 1903, sheds light on the historic moment when the deed transferring the majority of the property at Pacific City to the Huntington Beach Company, led by Henry E. Huntington, was filed. According to the report, the transaction took place with a purchase price of $95,000. The West Coast Land and Water Company, which had founded Pacific City approximately two years prior, completed the deal with Huntington's interests, making them the new owners of the beach property. This acquisition marked a significant turning point in the development of the area. The report also mentions that one of the planned improvements for the newly acquired property was the construction of an electric railroad to connect the resort. This development was indicative of Huntington's ambition to create easy access to the area and facilitate its growth as a desirable destination. The report also noted that the name "Huntington Beach" would be used to refer to the area going forward. This announcement in the press is believed to be the first official reference to the name "Huntington Beach" in public records.

The purchase and subsequent development of Pacific City by Henry E. Huntington and his team were instrumental in shaping the future of the region. The establishment of a new name, "Huntington Beach," marked the beginning of an era that would transform the area into a renowned coastal city and a popular tourist destination.

Then came the trains one year later.

Henry Huntington's electric Red Cars, arriving on July 4, 1904, marked a milestone in the city's transportation system. The trial period prior to that date allowed for testing and preparation for the official launch. The creation of the Huntington Beach Fourth of July parade on the same day has become

July 4, 1904, the first official day the trains came to Huntington Beach. *Author's collection.*

a long-standing tradition and a symbol of celebration for the city. Today, being considered the longest-running Independence Day parade west of the Mississippi is quite an accomplishment. The parade was designed to welcome the influx of visitors who came to the city for the first time, and it has continued to be a major event that holds a special place in the city's history. It's wonderful to see how a festive day and a massive celebration have endured over time and continue to be celebrated in the present day.

The arrival of the Pacific Electric trains also had a significant impact on the tourism industry in Huntington Beach. The trains brought visitors from all over Southern California to the city's beaches, which were some of the best in the region. Tourists flocked to the city to enjoy the sun, sand and surf, and local businesses thrived as a result. Hotels, restaurants and other tourist-related businesses sprung up to cater to the growing demand, and the city quickly became known as a premier vacation destination.

The trains also had a profound impact on the social fabric of Huntington Beach. Prior to their arrival, the city was a relatively insular community with limited opportunities for social interaction. The trains changed this by

Henry Huntington's Pacific Electric Red Cars ran right along the coast. *Author's collection.*

connecting Huntington Beach with nearby cities, making it easier for people to travel to and from social events and gatherings. The trains also brought people from different backgrounds and walks of life to the city, creating a more diverse and vibrant community.

In addition to their economic and social impacts, the Pacific Electric trains also helped shape the physical landscape of Huntington Beach. The trains brought with them new development opportunities, and local landowners quickly recognized the potential for growth and expansion. The arrival of the trains spurred a flurry of construction activity in the city, with new buildings, roads and infrastructure being built to accommodate the growing population.

Despite the many positive impacts of the Pacific Electric trains, however, their arrival was not without its challenges. The increased population and development brought by the trains put a strain on the city's resources, and local officials were forced to adapt quickly to meet the growing demand for services and infrastructure. In addition, the trains themselves were not without their problems, and accidents and delays were not uncommon. With the train tracks running literally in the sand near the shore, workers were constantly clearing sand away from the rails and dealing with high tide flooding. Even with these challenges, however, the Pacific Electric trains had a lasting impact on Huntington Beach that can still be felt today. The trains helped shape the city's identity and culture and played a crucial role in its development and growth. Today, the legacy of the Pacific Electric trains can be seen in the city's historic downtown area, as well as in the many tourist attractions and cultural institutions that have sprung up in the years since their arrival.

The introduction of the Red Cars, part of Henry Huntington's innovative train system, had a monumental impact on the development of Huntington Beach in the early 1900s. Prior to the Red Cars, traveling from Huntington Beach to Los Angeles was a time-consuming and arduous journey that often took two days by stagecoach. However, the advent of the Red Cars revolutionized transportation, reducing the travel time to a mere two hours.

This significant reduction in travel time brought about a transformation in the accessibility and connectivity of Huntington Beach to the rest of Southern California. It opened new opportunities for trade, commerce and tourism, fueling the growth and development of the area. The Red Cars not only facilitated the movement of people but also provided a convenient means of transporting goods and resources, contributing to the economic prosperity of the region.

One intriguing aspect of the Red Car system was the special stop created at the Bolsa Chica Gun Club. This stop was exclusively reserved for the club's members, and it required them to present a unique membership card signed by Henry Huntington himself. This special privilege further enhanced the exclusivity and prestige associated with the gun club, solidifying its status as a prominent destination for the wealthy and influential individuals of the time.

By providing a direct transportation link to the gun club, the Red Cars added a touch of convenience and luxury to the members' experience. It allowed them to seamlessly travel between Los Angeles and the club, saving them from the hassle and inconvenience of alternative modes of transportation. This unique feature not only bolstered the gun club's reputation but also contributed to its allure as a retreat for the affluent members seeking respite from the demands of city life.

The introduction of Henry Huntington's Red Car train system certainly had a profound impact on the development of Huntington Beach. By drastically reducing travel time between Huntington Beach and Los Angeles, it facilitated the growth of the region and stimulated economic opportunities. The inclusion of a special stop at the Bolsa Chica Gun Club, exclusively accessible to club members, added an element of exclusivity and luxury to the experience, further enhancing the gun club's reputation as a prestigious destination for the elite of that time. And once you arrived at the club, the best of everything awaited.

10
FARM-TO-TABLE SUSTAINABILITY

The Bolsa Chica Gun Club was known not only for its exclusive membership and recreational shooting activities but also for its pioneering approach to the farm-to-table concept. In an era when such practices were relatively uncommon for such an exclusive facility, the gun club took it upon itself to grow its own vegetables, raise poultry and even maintain cattle for milk production, ensuring that its wealthy clientele enjoyed fresh and locally sourced food.

The Bolsa Chica Gun Club's farm-to-table concept was not without challenges. The rugged coastal environment and its proximity to the ocean brought unique obstacles, including salty air, strong winds and limited access to water. However, the club's dedicated staff overcame these challenges through innovative farming techniques, such as implementing windbreaks and using and maximizing water conservation measures.

The farm-to-table practices employed by the Bolsa Chica Gun Club were ahead of their time. Long before the modern food movement highlighted the importance of locally sourced and sustainable ingredients, the gun club recognized the value of providing its members with the freshest and highest-quality food possible. By cultivating its own vegetables, raising poultry and maintaining cattle, the club ensured a level of culinary excellence that matched the exclusivity of its membership.

The farm-to-table concept embraced by the Bolsa Chica Gun Club became an integral part of its identity. Today, the legacy of the gun club's innovative approach to food sourcing serves as a reminder of the

The enclosure where birds were raised for food, circa 1902. *Author's collection.*

importance of quality, self-sufficiency and environmental stewardship in the culinary world. The Bolsa Chica Gun Club recognized the importance of self-sufficiency and quality in providing for its members. The club's idyllic coastal setting provided an opportunity to create a self-sustaining ecosystem that would cater to the culinary needs of its privileged clientele. With fertile land and a favorable climate, the gun club established its own farm and livestock operations.

The club's commitment to self-sufficiency began with the cultivation of vegetables. It employed skilled horticulturists and agricultural experts to develop and maintain a diverse range of crops. The club's farm boasted an array of seasonal vegetables, including leafy greens, root vegetables and a variety of herbs. By growing its own produce, the club ensured a steady supply of fresh, organic vegetables that would make their way to the dining tables of the membership. In addition to vegetables, the Bolsa Chica Gun Club also embraced animal husbandry. It raised chickens and pheasants to provide a reliable source of poultry for its members. The birds were

The enclosure where birds were raised for food, circa 1902. *Author's collection.*

carefully bred and raised on the club's grounds, allowing for a controlled and sustainable supply of high-quality meat. The gun club took pride in offering its members poultry products that were free from hormones and antibiotics, providing a truly farm-to-table experience.

The club also maintained a small herd of cattle to meet the demand for fresh milk. The cows grazed on the lush coastal pastures, ensuring the milk produced was of the highest quality. Members could enjoy fresh milk, cream and other dairy products straight from the club's own cows, adding to the exclusivity of their dining experience.

A FAMOUS CLUB RECIPE

The Castelar Creche, a home for homeless babies in Los Angeles during the 1920s to the 1950s, holds a significant place in the city's history. In the 1920s, the home produced historic cookbooks as a means of soliciting patrons to support the home. During one particular year, the Bolsa Chica Gun Club contributed a special recipe to the cookbook, featuring a beloved dish known as chicken terrapin. The recipe provided by the Bolsa Chica Gun Club showcased a flavorful and indulgent preparation. The recipe called for dark meat chicken, which was cooked in a casserole dish. To enhance the taste, the chicken was seasoned with salt, pepper, cayenne pepper, parsley, onion juice and chicken juice. These ingredients added depth and richness to the dish. Additionally, a couple of beaten eggs were incorporated into the recipe, likely to provide texture and richness. To complement the flavors even further, a sherry sauce was included, adding a touch of sophistication and complexity to the dish.

The contribution of the chicken terrapin recipe by the Bolsa Chica Gun Club to the Castelar Creche cookbook represented more than just a culinary creation. It symbolized the community's support for the home and its commitment to caring for the vulnerable and homeless babies in Los Angeles. With that said, amid the rugged escapism, great food and drink and male bonding, a war was brewing.

11

THE WAR WITH THE FARMERS

{ tarting in 1901, a war of sorts broke out between the farmers in the Huntington Beach area and the elite members of the Bolsa Chica Gun Club. The conflict arose when the gun club sealed off the Freeman River (also called "Freeman Creek"), which meant the farmers wouldn't have the same access to the ocean. This sparked a bitter feud that lasted for several years and had far-reaching consequences for both sides.

The Freeman River, which once ran through the gun club property and into the Pacific Ocean, was an important source of water for local farmers. The river provided irrigation for their crops and allowed them to transport goods to market via the ocean. However, in 1901, the Bolsa Chica Gun Club decided to build a dam across the river to create a private lagoon for its members. The dam effectively cut off the farmers' access to the ocean, which caused outrage and frustration among the farming community. The gun club's decision to seal off the river was seen as a blatant disregard for the needs of the local farmers, who were struggling to make a living in a difficult economic climate. The farmers were determined to fight back against the gun club and began a campaign to have the dam removed. They argued that the dam was not only unfair but also illegal, as it was blocking a navigable waterway. The farmers filed a lawsuit against the gun club.

The Westminster Farmers Club was formed as an organization to represent the interests of the farmers affected by the dam. Recognizing that the gun club's actions infringed on their rights, the farmers filed a lawsuit against the club. The lawsuit was centered on the defense of the farmers' legal right to

Club members posing in front of the main house in the early 1900s. *Author's collection.*

utilize the river for commerce and navigation, which was protected under both state and federal constitutional law.

The concept of "the public trust" played a crucial role in the farmers' legal argument. The public trust doctrine, deeply rooted in common law, stipulates that certain resources, such as navigable waters, are held in trust by the government for the benefit of the public. This doctrine asserts that the public has the right to utilize these resources for purposes like commerce, navigation and recreation.

By obstructing the navigable waters and impeding the farmers' access to the shoreline, the Bolsa Chica Gun Club was potentially violating the farmers' rights protected under the public trust doctrine. The farmers' lawsuit aimed to challenge the club's actions and seek legal remedies to restore their access to Freeman Creek.

This is a letter that the farmers sent to the U.S. district attorney.

January 30, 1901
The honorary U.S. district attorney
Los Angeles California

Dear sir:

The Bolsa Chica Gun Club, a corporation, has placed obstructions in Bolsa Chica Inlet a natural Harbour of Orange County California which entirely closes it as a harbor for light sale and fishing boats. Bolsa Chica inlet being navigable water of the United States, this has been in violation of our national navigation laws. By so doing this said gun club has appropriated to their own private use the said inlet to the entire exclusion of the people from the same, not only as a harbor but also as a hunting and fishing ground. By shutting out the salt water valuable beds of oysters, clams and other varieties of saltwater shellfish have been destroyed and saltwater fish have died in large numbers. The stench arising has caused malaria and typhoid to an extent never before known in the vicinity. Moreover this said gun club has recently used this said obstruction to the positive damage of farming lands adjoining, by raising or backing up the water flowing into the said inlet from the Bolsa drainage ditch to such an extent that water is now standing in the furrows of plowed land. We earnestly request you take steps to have these obstructions speedily removed as the law directs. We make this complaint and request upon the advice of senator George C Perkins. Earnestly hoping that you will take prompt action in this matter for the relief of our people, we are very respectfully, Westminster farmers club.

The legal battle between the farmers and the gun club was fierce and bitter. However, despite the farmers' strong legal argument, their limited financial resources and the gun club's substantial influence posed significant obstacles. The gun club leveraged its wealth and connections to mount a strong defense, employing skilled lawyers and employing tactics to protect their interests.

The conflict between the farmers and the wealthy members of the Bolsa Chica Gun Club indeed took on a dramatic and tense quality, resembling a storyline from a movie. The farmers, armed with shotguns, would frequently venture onto the gun club's property, engaging in confrontations with the club's guards. Given the heightened emotions and stakes involved, it is remarkable these encounters did not result in regular bloodshed.

At the forefront of the farmers' resistance stood Dennis McGirk, a spirited and determined celery farmer. McGirk emerged as a legendary figure during the battle, admired for his unwavering commitment to the cause. Notably, he was not a hunter himself nor did he have any personal interest in the use of Freeman Creek. Instead, McGirk firmly believed that the gun club had wrongfully appropriated land that rightfully belonged to the United States government. His actions were driven entirely by his principled stance. McGirk's tenacity and unwavering dedication resonated with the farmers and the wider community. He became a symbol of resilience and defiance against the overwhelming power and wealth of the gun club members. McGirk's leadership galvanized the farmers and inspired them to continue their fight, despite the odds stacked against them. McGirk's commitment to the belief that the land belonged to the United States government underscored the importance of principles and justice in his fight. His

DENNIS M^c GIRK

Dennis McGirk, a celery farmer who led the charge against millionaires. *Author's collection.*

steadfast stance resonated with the farmers and helped sustain their resistance, even in the face of repeated challenges and setbacks.

While the farmers' excursions onto the gun club's property and their confrontations with guards demonstrated the intensity of the conflict, it is important to note that resorting to violence was not the desired outcome for either side. Both parties likely recognized the potential for tragedy in such circumstances and sought to avoid bloodshed. Nevertheless, the heightened tensions and clashes between the two groups painted a vivid picture of a community divided by competing interests and power dynamics.

Ultimately, the farmers' lawsuit faced an uphill battle. The court proceedings were protracted and costly, and the gun club's legal team skillfully countered the farmers' claims. Although the farmers were justified in their defense of their rights under the public trust doctrine, they were unable to overcome the gun club's power and influence. As a result, the gun club retained control over Freeman Creek, leaving the farmers and others who relied on the waterway for commerce and navigation at a significant disadvantage.

The farmers' struggle to protect their rights to use Freeman Creek for commerce and navigation against the Bolsa Chica Gun Club exemplifies the challenges faced by individuals and communities when confronted with well-funded and influential opponents. The conflict between the farmers and the Bolsa Chica Gun Club represented a clash of values and interests, magnified by the stark contrast in wealth and influence between the two groups. While the farmers' efforts were fueled by principles and a sense of justice, their struggle against the formidable power of the gun club members proved to be an uphill battle.

As one unnamed gun club member was quoted as saying in the *Los Angeles Times*, "There is no use of your kicking, we have got the most money and we are bound to win. When your money is all gone we will not even miss what we spend in this fight." And that member was correct. The farmers eventually even petitioned then-president Theodore Roosevelt, but to no avail. However, the legacy of figures like Dennis McGirk and the collective resistance of the farmers serve as a testament to the enduring spirit and

95

determination of those who fought for what they believed was right. The outcome of the struggle between the farmers and the Bolsa Chica Gun Club in the early 1900s serves as a poignant example of the immense power and influence that wealth can wield. Despite the farmers' spirited resistance and their deep connection to the land, they were ultimately no match for the financial resources and connections possessed by the gun club members. The loss of Freeman Creek to the gun club marked a significant blow to the farmers' way of life, depriving them of both agricultural resources and a cherished recreational area. They were disgruntled for decades over this. But what about the rest of the area? What did Huntington Beach residents think of the Bolsa Chica Gun Club?

12

HOW HUNTINGTON BEACH
VIEWED THE CLUB

As the city of Huntington Beach began to develop in the early 1900s, the Bolsa Chica Gun Club maintained an air of mystery. Situated outside the city's borders for many years, it felt like an untamed and unapproachable location.

While riding the Red Car, a popular mode of transportation back then, locals could catch glimpses of the gun club perched on the mesa. However, they had no idea what transpired within its grounds, adding to the air of secrecy and curiosity that surrounded it.

In later years, groups of adventurous boys, typically around twelve or thirteen years old, would seize the opportunity to embark on daring escapades. They would secretly board the early-morning Red Cars, their fathers' shotguns in tow. With a sense of excitement and trepidation, they would position themselves on the beach directly across from the club, eagerly waiting for the first blasts of gunfire at dawn.

As one of the then-boys, Leroy Jauman, described much later in life (as a ninety-year-old man), those initial shots would startle the birds congregated near the ocean. The sudden commotion would send flocks of birds into the sky, providing the boys with the chance for a clean shot. They would seize the moment, carefully aiming their borrowed shotguns, and successfully bring down several birds. With their prized catches in hand, the boys would triumphantly return home, their hearts brimming with the joy of adventure and the satisfaction of providing for their families. The birds they collected became a savory dinner, a testament to their resourcefulness and skilled marksmanship.

The allure of the Bolsa Chica Gun Club stemmed not only from its proximity to the city but also from the secrecy surrounding its activities. The fact that it remained beyond the city's reach for years only added to its enigmatic charm. The gunshots that echoed across the beach at dawn served as a call to those daring enough to venture out and hunt for their own sustenance.

Over time, as the city expanded and modernized, the mystique surrounding the gun club gradually faded away. The land was eventually integrated into the city's boundaries, and the once-wild area transformed into a more developed and regulated environment.

The tale of those young boys, their clandestine adventures and the bounty they brought home serves as a nostalgic reminder of a bygone era. It reflects a time when the boundaries between urban and rural spaces were more fluid, and the spirit of exploration and self-sufficiency thrived.

By the 1920s, the Bolsa Chica Gun Club began to transition from a mysterious and distant entity to a more familiar place for the locals of Huntington Beach. This change was partly due to the economic prosperity brought about by the local oil strikes. As oil was discovered and extracted in the region, it brought considerable wealth and development to the area. Some of the locals who benefited from these oil strikes found themselves in a newfound position of financial stability. With increased disposable income, they sought out recreational activities that were previously inaccessible to them.

The Bolsa Chica Gun Club, once shrouded in mystique, became an alluring option for these affluent locals. Many of them became members

Relaxing by the beach in the early 1900s. *Author's collection.*

of the club, enjoying the camaraderie and exclusive privileges it offered. Membership in the gun club provided an opportunity for socializing, networking and engaging in a popular pastime of the era—shooting and hunting.

The newfound familiarity between the locals and the Bolsa Chica Gun Club helped bridge the gap between the city and the once-remote area. As more people joined the club and shared their experiences with others, the club's activities and offerings became better known within the community. However, it's important to note that the transition from an exclusive and mysterious club to a more familiar institution did not diminish the allure of the gun club entirely. Instead, the club evolved into a respected establishment that played a significant role in the recreational and social lives of its members.

The local oil strikes not only brought financial prosperity but also facilitated a cultural shift in the area. The Bolsa Chica Gun Club became a symbol of the changing times, where locals could enjoy the benefits of their newfound wealth and engage in activities previously reserved for the privileged few. How did the rest of the world learn about what was going on at the club as the eras progressed? That was the media's job.

13

THE PRESS

I n the early 1900s, the newspapers were avidly engaged in capturing the essence of society's interests and events, and the Bolsa Chica Gun Club was no exception. With their journalistic prowess, reporters of all stripes found themselves captivated by the allure of the gun club, dedicating ample coverage across various sections of the newspaper.

In the news pages, the happenings at the Bolsa Chica Gun Club were meticulously chronicled. From the opening of the shooting season to the latest developments in shooting techniques, readers were kept well-informed of the club's activities. The journalists delved into the details of marksmanship competitions, reporting on the participants, their scores and the thrilling atmosphere that enveloped the gun club.

The society pages, with their elegant prose and enticing descriptions, painted a vivid picture of the social scene at the Bolsa Chica Gun Club. High-society gatherings, charity events held on its premises and the fashionable attendees were all meticulously documented. From the lavish costumes worn by the ladies to the dapper attire of the gentlemen, every detail was captured, enhancing the allure of the club within the minds of the readers.

Even the sports pages, typically dedicated to more traditional athletic pursuits, found themselves enthralled by the allure of the gun club. Reports on shooting competitions and feats of marksmanship were featured alongside accounts of baseball games and horse races. The skill, precision and strategy displayed by the shooters were celebrated, elevating shooting as a sport worthy of admiration.

Rumors and whispered tales of secret get-togethers and clandestine gatherings at the Bolsa Chica Gun Club also found their way into the newspapers. Speculation and intrigue surrounded these alleged events, fueling the curiosity of readers who eagerly devoured every morsel of gossip the journalists could uncover.

In this way, the newspapers of the early 1900s became the storytellers of the Bolsa Chica Gun Club, painting a vivid and captivating narrative for their readers. From the news pages to the society pages and even the sports pages, the reporters brought to life the essence of the club, ensuring that its allure and mystique captivated the imaginations of readers far and wide.

An article in the *Anaheim Gazette* from March 15, 1900, gave a good idea of what it took to actually physically get to the brand-new gun club. The headline read, "A picnic at the Seaside, Bolsa Chica Club Entertains Its Friends at the Club Grounds."

A special train run from Pasadena and Los Angeles conveys a jolly party to Smeltzer, where carriages take them to the clubhouse. A sumptuous lunch, shooting boating and fishing filled the day.

The Bolsa Chica Gun Club entertained its friends at a picnic at the club grounds on Saturday. A special train of five cars was run from Pasadena in Los Angeles, stopping at Buena Park, this city and Orange to take on members of the club and invited guests. 160 ladies and gentlemen composed the party, which was under the personal charge of Mr. Botsford, President of the Bolsa Chica land company and count von Schmidt, President of the gun club. An orchestra of 10 pieces accompanied the Excursion and discoursed music during the trip. In the afternoon it rendered music for a dance program in the main assembly hall of the spacious clubhouse were many couples tripped the light fantastic to the latest musical airs. At the clubhouse, the clink of glasses, of silver spoon upon China and the merry laughter of one of the jolliest crowds ever collected together in Orange County, filled the dining room. 10 superb roasted turkeys were in course of being discussed. There were other delicacies to [sic] numerous to mention, meats, imported cheese of various descriptions, relishes, salads, olives, cakes, pies, coffee, lemonade, beer and champagne.

The *Los Angeles Evening Express*, on October 19, 1899, ran a headline that read, "Formal Opening of the Clubhouse and Shooting Grounds in Orange County Tuesday. Best Quarters in Southern California."

The grounds of the club are situated south of Anaheim Landing and contain several hundred acres of the best duck feeding grounds in the state. At great expense the club recently erected a large dam across the channel connecting the sloughs with the ocean that's securing plenty of water for shooting purposes. The construction of this dam has raised a storm a [sic] *protest from some of the owners of peatlands in the southwestern part of Orange County, and the board of supervisors of the county have under consideration of petition for the removal of the dam. The ranchers contend that owing to the damn the water is backed up so as to flood their property. The new clubhouse on the shooting grounds is one of the finest of the state. It's* [sic] *exterior appearance is not attractive but the interior finish is on a scale end of a character that would do credit to almost any mansion. The interior is finished in polished redwood, and there are several immense brick fireplaces with huge andirons on which are burned whole sections of large trees. The house is built upon the style of the old English taverns and is commodious enough to accommodate have 100 guests.*

It is built around a great hall, a baronial affair, with a huge fireplace and the heads of fish and game about; there are pianos and organs and patent pianos: gun rooms with fowling pieces to make a lesser hundred kill himself with envy; Directors rooms, sleeping rooms for each member, library; sheds for the game to be home, a label to hook for each member. Back of the clubhouse is an aviary were [sic] *ducks of all kinds are living a team old age. In a pocket of the hills underneath the clubhouse cliff are the kennels and boat houses in the bunkhouses for the guards and the keepers.*

On June 29, 1916, an intriguing story made its way into the *Santa Ana Register*, capturing the attention of readers. It detailed an event that took place at the Bolsa Chica Gun Club, where Charles J. Andrews, the club's manager, displayed remarkable bravery.

The focal point of the story was Rattlesnake Island, a small island situated within the gun club's property. It was on this island that Andrews encountered two venomous rattlesnakes, leading to an unusual and daring feat.

According to the article, Andrews successfully killed both rattlesnakes, showcasing his fearlessness in the face of danger. The report noted that one of the reptiles measured an impressive three and a half feet in length, while the other was just six inches shorter. The sheer size of the snakes emphasized the magnitude of Andrews's achievement.

The story captivated readers, offering a thrilling glimpse into the adventures and challenges faced by those who frequented the gun club. It showcased the realities of living in a region that was home to various wildlife, including potentially dangerous creatures like rattlesnakes.

While the event itself may have seemed relatively small in the grand scheme of things, it exemplified the everyday encounters and triumphs that were part of life at the Bolsa Chica Gun Club. Such incidents provided a glimpse into the unique experiences and stories that unfolded within the club's grounds.

It was also not uncommon for journalists to keep a close watch on the game counts, providing the public with updates on the club's hunting achievements. One such instance occurred on November 10, 1906, when the *Santa Ana Register* reported that a significant number of ducks had been shot at the Bolsa Chica Gun Club since the opening of the duck season on October 15.

This report highlighted the club's active participation in hunting and showcased the success of its members in pursuing waterfowl. The figure of two thousand ducks being shot within a relatively short period was indicative of the club's skilled marksmen and the abundance of game in the Bolsa Chica area during that particular season.

For avid hunters and members of the gun club, such reports served as a measure of pride and accomplishment. The numbers reflected the collective efforts of the club's members, their hunting prowess and their ability to contribute to the local ecosystem through responsible hunting practices.

As well, the press coverage of the Bolsa Chica Gun Club's hunting activities allowed the wider community to stay informed about the region's hunting traditions and the impact of hunting seasons on local wildlife populations. It also highlighted the importance of conservation efforts and responsible game management, as the numbers reported would shed light on the sustainability and health of the waterfowl population.

In December 1941, a significant event was reported at the Bolsa Chica Gun Club, marking a progressive step forward in the club's history. For the first time, women were granted the opportunity to participate in shooting activities at the duck club, reflecting the changing times and evolving attitudes toward gender roles.

The man who managed the club, recognizing the shifting social norms, decided to introduce the idea of allowing women to shoot. It was seen as a novel and enjoyable concept, an opportunity for women to engage in an activity traditionally associated with men.

Although the records indicate that none of the women managed to reach their hunting limit, the club ensured that they were well taken care of. As they waited for ducks, the women were provided with a hearty lunch consisting of turkey hash and apple pic, an indulgent treat to enhance their shooting experience.

At the end of the day, a dinner was organized to celebrate this groundbreaking occasion. A special ceremony was held, honoring the women who became the first to participate in shooting activities at the club. The event served as a testament to the club's commitment to inclusivity and adaptability in the face of changing societal norms and was generously covered by the local papers, given the changes it seemed to signify.

As the evening progressed, the guests gathered around the living room hearth, creating a warm and inviting atmosphere. Bridge and domino games were played, fostering camaraderie and friendly competition among the attendees. These games provided an opportunity for everyone to socialize and enjoy each other's company, further enhancing the sense of community within the gun club.

The event, held in December 1941 at the Bolsa Chica Gun Club, not only marked a milestone for women's participation in shooting activities but also showcased the club's dedication to creating an inclusive and welcoming environment. It represented a shift in attitudes toward gender roles and highlighted the changing dynamics of the time, making it a great topic for enterprising reporters.

The press's enthusiasm for documenting the club's activities played a significant role in raising public awareness and interest in the Bolsa Chica Gun Club. Through their coverage, journalists helped establish the club's reputation and fostered a sense of excitement and curiosity among readers. However, an event took place in 1910 that gave the press perhaps their greatest local story for the entire decade.

14

HUBERT LATHAM

Hubert Latham was a French aviator and aviation pioneer who made significant contributions to the early development of powered flight. While he didn't achieve the same level of fame as some of his contemporaries, such as the Wright brothers or Louis Blériot, Latham's flight history is still noteworthy and exciting.

One of Latham's most famous attempts took place on July 19, 1909, during the early days of aviation. He aimed to become the first person to cross the English Channel by air, a feat that had eluded many other aviators at the time. Latham flew a monoplane called the *Antoinette IV*, designed and built by Léon Levavasseur.

As Latham ventured into the skies, he encountered numerous challenges. Only a few miles into his flight, his aircraft experienced engine trouble, and he was forced to make an emergency landing in the sea, thus becoming the first person to ever land on water. Despite this setback, Latham displayed great determination and made multiple subsequent attempts in the following weeks.

On July 25, 1909, Latham's perseverance paid off. He took off from Sangatte, France, and headed toward Dover, England. However, about halfway through the flight, at an altitude of approximately nine hundred feet, his engine failed again. Undeterred, Latham performed a controlled emergency landing on the water, where he was rescued by a French destroyer.

Latham's channel crossing attempts brought him considerable recognition and cemented his place in aviation history. Although he didn't achieve the

French aviator Hubert Latham.
Author's collection.

successful flight he had hoped for, his daring spirit and determination inspired other aviators to continue pushing the boundaries of flight.

Beyond his English Channel endeavors, Latham also made noteworthy flights in other parts of the world. In 1909, he set an altitude record by flying to an impressive height of 4,541 feet in Châlons, France. He also participated in various aviation competitions and races, showcasing his skill and passion for flight.

Hubert Latham's contributions to aviation, particularly his attempts to cross the English Channel, played a significant role in advancing the field of aviation and inspiring future aviators. His adventurous spirit and determination in the face of challenges continue to be celebrated in the history of early aviation.

One of the most famous airshows held in Southern California in December 1910 was the Dominguez Air Meet. The event took place in Dominguez Hills, near Los Angeles, and it marked a significant milestone in the history of aviation in the region. During the airshow, spectators witnessed a range of aviation feats and demonstrations. Aviators showcased their skills in various aircraft, including biplanes, monoplanes and dirigibles. They performed daring stunts, such as loop-the-loops, barrel rolls, and high-speed flights. The event also included competitions, including races and altitude challenges, adding an element of excitement and competition to the airshow. The Dominguez Air Meet drew massive crowds, with estimates ranging from 175,000 to 250,000 attendees over the course of the event. It was one of the largest aviation gatherings of its time, and the enthusiasm and fascination for flight were palpable among the spectators.

The airshow not only provided entertainment but also played a significant role in promoting aviation and stimulating public interest. It showcased the potential of aviation technology and its future applications, which had a lasting impact on the development of aviation in Southern California.

The Dominguez Air Meet also marked the first time that an airplane flew over Los Angeles, capturing the imagination of the city's residents and further fueling the public's fascination with flight. The event paved the way for future airshows and aviation advancements in the region.

In December 1910, the nation became captivated by the incredible achievement of famed French aviator Hubert Latham. The excitement

). 307.   **TOPEKA, K**

HUBERT LATHAM GOES DUCK HUNTING IN HIS AEROPLANE--OUTFLIES DUCKS

Los Angeles, Dec. 22.—Hubert Latham, the noted French aviator, went duck hunting today at the Bolsa Chico Gun club in his fast Antoinette monoplane. He circled over the feeding grounds of the wild fowls, driving his machine at a high rate of speed and frightening the birds into the air in droves of thousands. With a double barreled shot gun Latham fired ten times at the ducks, killing a few and crippling others.

After pursuing the sport for more than half an hour Latham landed successfully at the club house.

The sight of the aviator circling over the marshes and driving swarms of birds into the air, now and then releasing control of his machine to grasp his gun and fire at them, was one of the most novel ever witnessed. A group of invited guests of the gun club stood on a knoll overlooking the shooting grounds, and watched the sport of the air man.

Carrying his loaded shotgun across his lap the aviator sat quietly in his machine as he approached the shooting grounds. Once in the vicinity of the marshes thousands of water fowl of all descriptions arose quacking and squawking, frightened by the appearance of this strange aerial monster.

As the first flock left the water, Latham fired at the ducks nearest him. A few dropped to the water, and thousands more arose in all directions.

The aviator veered his machine and pursued a flock of big ducks that was making for safety toward the ocean. Flying directly over the club house Latham chased them out to sea, pursuing them more than three miles. In his swift machine he overtook and passed many of the slow denizens of the air.

The whole kingdom of water fowl seemed terrorized by the appearance of the big black monoplane with its broad, extended white wings and chugging motor.

News coverage of Hubert Latham's feat. *From the* Los Angeles Times.

that swept across the country was unparalleled when Latham became the very first man to shoot a bird while flying a plane. This historic event took place at the Bolsa Chica Gun Club, after members of the club issued a daring challenge to Latham during the famed Dominguez Air Meet near Los Angeles on December 22, 1910.

The genesis of this whimsical endeavor lay in the fertile imagination of John B. Miller, a member of both the illustrious gun club and the esteemed Dominguez Aero Park Aviation Committee. With a mischievous glint in his eye, Miller approached Latham, presenting him with an audacious proposition: to be the first aviator to shoot down a bird while soaring amid the clouds. Perhaps it was the allure of the unprecedented or simply Latham's maverick spirit, but to everyone's astonishment, he accepted the challenge.

Again, Hubert Latham was already a renowned figure in the world of aviation. Known for his fearless spirit and pioneering flights, Latham had

AVIATOR DEFEATS BIRDS IN A RACE

Just Going for Little Spin, Says Latham at Start of Remarkable Flight

NO ACCIDENTS TO MAR FEAT

Novel Hunt Preceded by a Fast Trip to Grounds of Bolsa Chica Gun Club

(Continued from Page One)

almost drowned the chug of the aeroplane's propellor as they soared away. Latham again tried for a bag, but failed. He was successful, however, in landing his second bird just as he left the field on his return trip to the aviation park.

After completing a detour of the marshes Latham brought his machine to the ground on a knoll a quarter of a mile from the Bolsa Chica club house and was met, as he stepped from the aeroplane, by a member of the club.

"I've had a fine hunt, thank you," he said to John B. Miller of the aviation committee. "I think next time I'll be able to do much better."

A search was instituted for the duck shot by the aviator and it was found floating near the ocean's edge. The duck proved to be a bluebill of the scaup or canvasback family, and weighed two and a half pounds.

While the search for the duck was going on Latham was the guest of the club at breakfast.

Members of the aviation committee and of the gun club congratulated Latham on his flight. For half an hour they had looked on at the strangest sight ever offered them—that of a man chasing birds.

GOES TWO MILES OVER OCEAN

Snapshot of Hubert Latham and His Antoinette in Pursuit of Ducks Above the Surf Near Bolsa Chica

LATHAM HUNTING DUCKS WITH MONOPLANE

News coverage of Hubert Latham's feat. *From the* Los Angeles Times.

captured the imagination of people worldwide. His previous attempts to cross the English Channel had garnered international attention, even though they fell short of success. It was this bold reputation that led the members of the Bolsa Chica Gun Club to issue their extraordinary challenge to Latham.

The news of the challenge quickly spread throughout the country, sparking a sense of anticipation and wonder among aviation enthusiasts and the general public alike. The prospect of witnessing a man shooting a bird while flying a plane was unprecedented and captured the collective imagination of the nation. The event promised to be a remarkable display of skill, precision and audacity.

On the appointed day, as Latham soared through the sky in his aircraft, spectators gathered at the Bolsa Chica Gun Club in eager anticipation. The atmosphere was electric, with a mix of excitement, curiosity and awe hanging in the air. People from all walks of life, from aviation enthusiasts to casual observers, had come together to witness this historic moment.

As Latham descended toward the gun club, the tension reached its peak. All eyes were fixed on the aviator, waiting for the precise moment when he would take aim and attempt to shoot a bird while piloting his plane. The sound of the aircraft's engine filled the air, drowning out the murmurs of the crowd. Anticipation mounted with each passing second.

News spread like wildfire through the small community, and anticipation reached a feverish pitch. The mesa, overlooking the gun club, became a buzzing hive of activity. A curious amalgamation of gun club members, media personnel and intrigued onlookers gathered, their gazes fixed on the vast expanse of the eastern sky.

Then, as if summoned by destiny itself, a tiny speck emerged from the horizon. The crowd erupted into exultant cheers, for they recognized it as Latham's distinctive aircraft, the resplendent *Antoinette*. With graceful finesse, Latham descended from the heavens, his plane gently alighting on the meticulously manicured lawn before the gun club.

As he stepped out onto the verdant green, the aviator was handed a specially crafted .20-caliber rifle, a testament to the unconventional nature of the impending feat. With steely determination in his eyes, Latham took to the skies once more, his propeller slicing through the air with a resolute purpose.

The daring pilot soared through the azure canvas, his nimble aircraft startling herds of grazing cattle on the outskirts of the gun club. With each maneuver, he pursued his feathered quarry, locked in a dance of aerial pursuit. The wind whispered secrets to him, as if conspiring to make history on this extraordinary day.

Then, in a moment that defied expectations, Latham's keen eyes spotted his avian adversary—a bird of majestic beauty, soaring effortlessly against the backdrop of the boundless sky. Time seemed to stand still as the aviator steadied his aim, his finger gently caressing the trigger. In a fraction of a heartbeat, the shot rang out, a resounding echo of triumph.

The bird, startled by the sudden intrusion into its ethereal realm, gracefully spiraled downward, a symbol of Latham's improbable victory. Cheers erupted from the crowd below, mingling with the symphony of wind and wings. Hubert Latham, the intrepid aviator, had etched his name in the annals of aviation as the first to accomplish this audacious feat.

The accounts published in the *Breeder and Sportsman of California* also provide a thrilling narrative of Hubert Latham's pursuit to become the first person to shoot a bird from an airplane. According to these firsthand accounts, the chase lasted for approximately fifteen minutes and was filled with dramatic twists and challenges.

Latham's airplane soared along the coast, with the birds flying in a state of confusion and uncertainty, attempting to evade the colossal machine pursuing them. The birds seemed disoriented, unsure of which direction to take in order to escape the perceived monster in the sky. This description paints a vivid picture of Latham's aerial pursuit and the reaction of the birds to the unfamiliar and threatening presence of an airplane.

However, Latham's shooting ability was hindered by the design of his aircraft. The propeller blades of his plane were located directly in front of his seat, creating a visual obstruction and limiting his range of motion. As a result, Latham had to maneuver himself halfway around or position the plane beneath the ducks in order to take a shot. This added a layer of complexity to the already challenging task of shooting birds in flight.

Whenever Latham managed to close the distance between his plane and the flock of birds, they would instinctively rise higher above him and change direction, making it difficult for him to get within effective shooting range. This behavior showcases the birds' natural instincts in response to perceived threats, utilizing their aerial agility to outmaneuver Latham's pursuit.

As the chase continued, the flock of birds eventually made a decisive move toward the ocean, perhaps seeking refuge or a less accessible area for Latham to follow. At this point, Latham redirected his attention to the nearby marshes. Stirring up thousands of birds in the marshes provided Latham with a relatively easier opportunity to take a shot, as the birds were in closer proximity and potentially less able to evade his pursuit.

And then it happened. With steady hands and unwavering focus, Latham spotted a bird flying nearby. Seizing the opportunity, he skillfully aimed his weapon and fired. The crack of the gunshot echoed through the air as the bird plummeted to the ground. A collective gasp of astonishment and applause erupted from the crowd as they witnessed this extraordinary feat.

The news of Latham's accomplishment spread like wildfire. Newspaper headlines throughout the country blazed with excitement, proclaiming the aviation milestone. People from coast to coast marveled at the audacity and skill demonstrated by the French aviator. Latham's achievement symbolized the triumph of human ingenuity and the limitless possibilities of aviation.

The event marked a turning point in the public perception of aviation. It showcased the potential for aerial exploration and the skill required to navigate the skies. Latham's accomplishment inspired a new generation of aviators and ignited a renewed passion for flight. It also highlighted the rapid progress being made in aviation technology, as planes became more capable and pilots pushed the boundaries of what was considered possible.

In the years that followed, Latham's achievement would be remembered as a pivotal moment in aviation history. The daring act of shooting a bird while flying a plane became a symbol of human endeavor and the indomitable spirit of exploration. Latham's name would forever be associated with this remarkable feat, solidifying his place in the annals of aviation and securing his legacy as a pioneer in the field.

The excitement that gripped the nation in December 1910 was palpable and long-lasting. It became a topic of conversation at dinner tables, in cafés and among friends. People marveled at the audacity and skill of Hubert Latham, discussing the event with great enthusiasm and admiration.

The achievement also had a profound impact on the perception of aviation as a whole. It served as a potent reminder of the rapid progress being made in this new field and fueled the public's imagination regarding the limitless possibilities of flight. The daring act of shooting a bird while flying a plane showcased the potential for aerial exploration and the courage required to push the boundaries of what was considered possible.

The media played a significant role in amplifying the excitement. Newspaper articles described the event in vivid detail, capturing the spectacle and the awe-inspiring nature of Latham's accomplishment. Photographs and illustrations accompanied these stories, allowing readers to visualize the historic moment. The headlines themselves were enough to generate buzz and intrigue, ensuring that the news reached even the most remote corners of the country.

In the aftermath of Latham's feat, interest in aviation soared. People became more captivated by the possibilities of flight, and aviation events drew larger crowds than ever before. The public's fascination with aviators and their daring exploits grew, and Latham became a revered figure. His name became synonymous with courage, skill and the pursuit of the impossible.

Beyond its immediate impact, Latham's achievement also had lasting implications for the development of aviation. It inspired other aviators to push the boundaries of what was deemed achievable, leading to further advancements in technology and flight techniques. The event sparked a wave of innovation and experimentation, as pilots sought to surpass Latham's feat and break new records.

Looking back, it's easy to see why the excitement that swept across the country in December 1910, when Hubert Latham became the first man to shoot a bird while flying a plane, was unparalleled.

Incidentally, of the two ducks he shot, which were recovered on the beach, one was served to him as his lunch, and the other he brought with him and eventually had stuffed as a trophy to commemorate this remarkable day. The duck is still in one of the Latham family homes in the

French countryside, and as of this writing, this author has been in touch with family representatives to see if they would consider shipping the duck back to Huntington Beach. Latham himself died two years later in Africa after he was mauled by a wounded buffalo. Latham's exploits at the gun club brought much attention—but nothing like what would occur about ten years later.

15

OIL!

By 1901, the Los Angeles area had become a thriving hub for oil production. Over nine hundred oil wells were operating in and around Los Angeles, making it one of the most productive oil regions in the United States. The oil industry brought significant economic growth and attracted many investors, leading to a boom in oil exploration and drilling activities.

In Orange County, the first successful oil well was drilled in 1882 near the town of Olinda, which is now known as Brea. This marked the beginning of oil production in Orange County. The discovery of oil in Brea brought about a transformation in the region, leading to the establishment of oil fields and the growth of the oil industry.

The success of the oil well in Brea spurred further exploration and drilling efforts in Orange County, leading to the discovery of additional oil reserves. Oil production became a vital part of the local economy and played a significant role in shaping the development of Orange County.

The opening of the first commercial oil field in California near Valencia in 1876, followed by the proliferation of oil wells around the Los Angeles area by 1901 and the successful oil well in Brea in 1882, marked significant milestones in the history of the oil industry in California, contributing to the state's economic growth and development.

The Bolsa Chica Wetlands received a plentiful supply of fresh water from the Freeman River. However, the source of this fresh water was primarily farm runoff, which rendered it unsuitable for drinking and cooking purposes. Recognizing the need for potable water, the Bolsa Chica Gun Club had a well dug near the clubhouse, hoping to find a suitable source of drinking water.

To the club's surprise, when it tested the water from the well, it discovered it was saturated with natural gas. Realizing the water was not fit for consumption, the club's members decided to separate the gas from the water. They found a practical use for the natural gas by utilizing it for cooking and lighting in the clubhouse and other outbuildings. This discovery provided the gun club with a convenient and cost-effective energy source.

However, despite its innovative solution for utilizing the natural gas, the club still faced the challenge of securing a reliable source of drinking water. As a result, it had to import drinking water by piping it in from external sources.

In 1916, rumors began circulating about the potential presence of oil beneath Huntington Beach, California. These rumors reached the officials of Standard Oil Company, who recognized the opportunity and decided to investigate further. The company approached the Huntington Beach Company, which owned a significant portion of the city, and secured a lease for the mineral rights on five hundred acres of land around the Golden West and Clay Streets area.

In August 1920, an exploratory well was drilled in the leased area, and to the delight of the oil company, it started producing a modest but promising seventy barrels of oil per day. This well was named Huntington Beach No. 1, signifying the beginning of oil production in the area. Encouraged by the initial success, the oil company decided to move its drilling equipment to the upper edge of the Huntington Mesa, which was located within the Bolsa Chica Gun Club property. Under a lease agreement with the gun club, drilling operations began.

On November 6, 1920, as the drillers reached a depth of 2,549 feet, a gusher erupted, causing a massive outpouring of oil. The force was so powerful that the well connections were blown off with a thunderous roar that could be heard for miles around. Within just twenty-four hours, an estimated twenty thousand barrels of oil covered the ground surrounding the well. This remarkable discovery quickly gained attention, and the well was named Bolsa Chica No. 1.

The production from Bolsa Chica No. 1 rapidly increased, reaching a peak of two thousand barrels of oil per day. The success of the well marked a significant milestone in the development of the oil industry in Huntington Beach, as it confirmed the presence of substantial oil reserves in the area.

The discovery of oil in Huntington Beach sparked a boom in oil exploration and production, attracting numerous oil companies and investors to the region. It brought significant economic growth and transformed the landscape and fortunes of the city.

In the aftermath of the initial gusher at the Bolsa Chica Wetlands, multiple oil companies saw the potential for profitable oil production in the area. Recognizing that the Bolsa Chica Gun Club held significant influence over the fate of the lowlands, these companies embarked on a campaign to convince the club members to lease a major portion of the land for oil production.

The oil companies approached the club members with lucrative offers, highlighting the financial benefits they would receive in exchange for leasing the land. They emphasized the potential wealth that could be generated from oil drilling and the substantial royalties that would be paid to the club.

It is worth mentioning that the Bolsa Chica Gun Club had already entered into an agreement in 1922 with Standard Oil to allow oil production on the mesa. At that time, the club had been enticed by a $100,000 bonus offered by Standard Oil for signing the lease, along with a 16⅔ percent royalty. However, this oil production on the mesa was located far enough from the wetlands that it did not interfere with the hunting activities taking place there.

Despite their previous agreement with Standard Oil, the club members were resolute in their decision to protect the wetlands from further industrialization.

By 1940, the economic conditions of many Bolsa Chica Gun Club members had been severely impacted by the stock market crash of 1929 and the subsequent Great Depression. The financial hardships they faced made the prospect of collecting additional oil royalties too enticing to ignore. Consequently, the club decided to approach Standard Oil with an offer to lease the lowlands for drilling on the condition that the oil company would raise the royalty rate from 16⅔ percent to 25 percent.

However, Standard Oil considered the proposition too risky. It believed that much of the oil in the area had already been depleted, making further drilling less profitable. Despite Standard Oil's hesitation, Signal Oil, a company that held a more optimistic outlook on the potential oil reserves, stepped in and made an offer to the club. Signal Oil proposed a royalty rate of 36 percent, along with 50 percent of net profits, in exchange for permission to drill in the lowland area of the wetlands.

In June 1940, a lease agreement was signed between Signal Oil and the Bolsa Chica Gun Club, allowing Signal Oil to drill twenty-two wells on 110 acres of the wetlands. This marked the beginning of the oil company's operations in the area. Recognizing the potential wealth that lay beneath the surface, many of the gun club members saw an opportunity to recapture their lost wealth and improve their economic circumstances.

The success of Signal Oil's drilling operations and the subsequent oil production proved to be fruitful for both the company and the club members. In 1943, a second lease was signed, expanding Signal's operations to an additional nine hundred acres of the lowlands.

As a result, many of the Bolsa Chica Gun Club members were able to regain their financial stability and wealth through the increased oil royalties and profits generated by the drilling activities. The decision to allow drilling in the wetlands provided a much-needed economic boost to the club members who had been adversely affected by the stock market crash and the Great Depression.

The discovery of oil in Huntington Beach and the tapping of wells in the Bolsa Chica Wetlands is a story of exploration, innovation and environmental impact. It is a tale that spans over a century and has shaped the economic and ecological landscape of Southern California. It made the gun club even more famous. And speaking of fame, there was a time when Hollywood rolled into the gun club.

16

THE BOLSA CHICA GUN CLUB ON FILM

Hollywood came to the Bolsa Chica Gun Club in 1930 with the Paramount Pictures production of *Sarah and Son,* a drama starring Ruth Chatterton and Frederic March, based on Timothy Shea's novel of the same name. The story follows the life of Sarah (Chatterton), a music hall singer whose husband steals their baby and the quest she embarks on to find her son.

Sarah and Son is a well-crafted drama that showcases the talents of its cast. It remains a notable example of early sound-era filmmaking. Interestingly, the movie was helmed by Dorothy Arzner, an American film director who had a Hollywood career extending from the silent era of the 1920s to the early 1940s. With the exception of the long-serving silent film director Lois Weber, who directed *White Heat* in 1934, Arzner was the sole female director working in Hollywood from 1927 until her retirement from feature directing in 1943. Throughout this time, Arzner created a total of twenty films, propelling the careers of several Hollywood actresses, such as Katharine Hepburn, Rosalind Russell and Lucille Ball. Arzner holds the distinction of being the first woman to join the Directors Guild of America and the first woman to direct a sound film.

The film affords some remarkable views of the Bolsa Chica Gun Club in 1930. Several scenes depict fancy cars pulling up the main driveway from Coast Highway and then curving around the expansive and well-manicured front lawn to park in front of the main large house. As well, there are many tighter shots shot along the clubhouse's primary structure, which give the viewer an up-close look at the intricate detail and craft work that went into the design and architecture of the club.

A scene from the 1930s film *Sarah and Son*. *Author's collection.*

The scarcity of footage shot at the Bolsa Chica Gun Club, combined with the fact that portions of the 1930 film *Sarah and Son* were shot there, makes the film particularly significant and valuable. This unique occurrence holds importance due to the lasting and important images it provides, offering a glimpse into the historical context and atmosphere of the gun club during that era.

Hollywood has played a pivotal role in shaping American popular culture and has created countless iconic images over the years. When Hollywood ventures into a specific location for filming, it often brings attention and recognition to that place, preserving its memory in the collective consciousness.

By featuring the gun club in *Sarah and Son*, the filmmakers inadvertently captured the essence and atmosphere of the location during that period. The film serves as a visual time capsule, presenting a window into the past and offering insights into the social, cultural and architectural aspects of the gun club. These images can provide valuable historical references, preserving the memory of the gun club in a way that cannot be replicated. And Ruth Chatterton received a Best Actress Academy Award® nomination for her role in the film (her second nomination after 1929's *Madame X*).

In 1939, some amateur film—not for Hollywood production—was shot at the Bolsa Chica Gun Club. It was filmed for a men's group called the Sunset Club, which clearly commissioned someone to shoot quality film, most likely 16 millimeter, and about nine minutes of it exists. The stunning and beautiful film depicts men at the gun club playing horseshoes, sharing drinks and relaxing.

The existence of limited photographs of the Bolsa Chica Gun Club, juxtaposed with the remarkable 16 millimeter color footage of the Sunset Club in 1939, provides a unique perspective on the club's activities and ambiance during that time. The footage offers valuable insights into the daily experiences and social dynamics of the club's members.

The fact that the footage captures moments of camaraderie, high spirits and enjoyment among the men of the Sunset Club indicates that the gun club had evolved into more than just a shooting range.

While photographs can provide snapshots of specific moments, the film offers a more immersive experience by capturing several minutes of continuous action. This allows viewers to witness the atmosphere, interactions and details that may have been missed in still images. The color

A scene from the rare 1939 color film shot by the Sunset Club. *Author's collection.*

A scene from the rare 1939 color film shot by the Sunset Club. *Author's collection.*

aspect of the footage further enhances the viewing experience, providing a vivid representation of the club and its surroundings as they appeared in the late 1930s.

While it is regrettable that there are only limited photographs available, the existence of this remarkable 16 millimeter footage compensates to a certain extent. It gives researchers, historians and individuals interested in the history of the Bolsa Chica Gun Club a valuable resource to study and appreciate the club's past, offering a more comprehensive and immersive perspective than static images alone. The color footage also represents the calm before the storm, as within just a couple of years, things would change dramatically. In fact, the members would no longer have control of their own club. The world and, along with it, the Bolsa Chica Gun Club were changing.

17

THE MILITARY

Following the assault on Pearl Harbor on December 7, 1941, the U.S. Army acquired the Bolsa Chica lands through fee, leasehold and permissions from fourteen parties during World War II. The War Department planned to build an artillery battery to defend Fort MacArthur and the nearby Port of Long Beach. On the northern side of the Bolsa Chica site, a number of structures were built, including fortifications, personnel and ammunition storage, gun emplacements, water tanks and towers, transformer vaults, two subterranean tanks, electrical and water utility systems and water tanks. On the hill above Outer Bolsa Bay, long-range gun emplacements were also built. On the northern end of the biological reserve, close to the tide gates, are the remains of one of these emplacements.

During World War II, the transformation of the Bolsa Chica Gun Club into a military barracks by the U.S. Army brought significant changes to the lives of the soldiers stationed there. Following the attack on Pearl Harbor, the army's concern about potential further attacks from the sea led them to take over strategic locations such as the gun club, which offered a vantage point overlooking the Pacific Ocean. Despite the absence of actual attacks, the soldiers stationed at the bluff experienced a unique and relatively uneventful military life in the mid-1940s.

The decision to establish a battery at the Bolsa Chica Gun Club was due to its strategic location along the coast. The lower lagoon level provided an advantageous position for defense, allowing for enhanced surveillance and protection against potential enemy threats approaching from the sea.

To accommodate the military presence, the gun club's clubhouse was repurposed as a temporary barracks for the soldiers stationed there. The clubhouse served as a living and administrative space, providing the necessary facilities and accommodations for the military personnel.

Construction activities began even before all the property was formally acquired. The military wasted no time in establishing a strong defense infrastructure. In addition to the temporary mobile battery, two modern larger-caliber gun batteries were constructed on a higher mesa overlooking the lagoon within the gun club's reservation. These batteries were designed to provide enhanced firepower and defense capabilities.

Other structures were also established on the reservation to support the gun batteries. An underground plotting switchboard radio structure was built specifically for battery no. 128. This structure served as a central hub for coordinating and directing artillery fire. Furthermore, a reserve ammunition magazine was constructed to store and supply the necessary ammunition for the batteries. This ensured a steady and readily available stock of ammunition for the defense installations.

A fire control tower was erected to provide an elevated vantage point for observing and directing artillery fire. This tower allowed the military personnel to monitor the coastline and coordinate their actions effectively. Additionally, a radar installation was established on the reservation. Radar technology played a crucial role in detecting and tracking enemy aircraft, providing early warnings and contributing to the overall defense strategy of the area.

The establishment of these structures and installations at the Bolsa Chica Gun Club demonstrated the military's commitment to fortifying the coastal defenses during World War II. The location's proximity to the ocean made it an ideal site for the placement of gun batteries and other defense structures. The presence of these facilities and the military personnel stationed there contributed to the overall defense of the region, ensuring the safety and security of the surrounding areas.

Additionally, the army initiated the installation of a 26-inch long-range gun farther up on the mesa in 1943. This construction project was concluded the following year. In 1943, the groundwork for mounting 216-inch cannons was also initiated. However, for reasons unknown, the guns were never installed.

These measures were taken to bolster the defense of the Bolsa Chica site during World War II. The placement of the 155-mm field guns and the construction of the larger guns were intended to enhance the site's artillery capabilities and provide a defensive position against potential threats.

Following the conclusion of World War II, the process of removing artillery guns and other structures from the Bolsa Chica Gun Club property and returning it to the club owners began.

The bunkers that were created on the property of the Bolsa Chica Gun Club during the war indeed hold near mythical status today. Built by the army corps of engineers primarily in 1944, these structures were part of an elaborate defense system. Among them was a massive bunker measuring 600 by 175 feet, designed to accommodate large artillery placements at either end. It also contained extensive storage areas for live ammunition and provided sleeping quarters for the intended crew.

However, after the war ended, the bunkers were abandoned and left empty. This left them open to exploration by locals, contributing to their legendary status. Over the years, these bunkers became a source of fascination and curiosity for those interested in military history and abandoned structures. They served as tangible reminders of the wartime era and offered a glimpse into the past.

The soldiers stationed at the Bolsa Chica barracks enjoyed several advantages due to its coastal location. The stunning views of the ocean provided a serene and picturesque backdrop for their daily lives. The constant ocean breezes helped create a cool and refreshing atmosphere, offering some respite from the Southern California heat. The natural beauty of the surroundings, combined with the pleasant climate, contributed to a more positive and enjoyable experience for the soldiers.

While military life during wartime is typically marked by intense training, combat and the hardships of war, the soldiers stationed at the Bolsa Chica barracks experienced a relatively calm period. The absence of actual attacks or combat situations allowed for a more peaceful existence. The soldiers focused on training, maintaining readiness and carrying out their assigned duties.

The barracks itself provided the soldiers with the necessary infrastructure and facilities for daily living. They had access to basic accommodations, mess halls for meals, recreational areas and other amenities to support their well-being. The military structure and routines were still in place, with soldiers adhering to strict schedules, participating in drills and undergoing training exercises to maintain their readiness for potential threats.

Despite the relatively uneventful nature of their military service, the soldiers stationed at the Bolsa Chica barracks were not devoid of entertainment and diversion. The United Service Organizations (USO) played a vital role in boosting morale for the troops during World War II. The occasional USO shows would be brought in to entertain the soldiers, providing them with live music, comedy acts and other forms of entertainment. These shows offered a welcome break from the routine and served as a reminder of the support and appreciation from the home front.

During World War II, the entire city of Huntington Beach experienced a significant military presence due to its strategic location along the coast. The Bolsa Chica Gun Club was not the only site where the army had a strong presence; various other locations throughout the city were utilized for military purposes.

One notable example was the transformation of the iconic Huntington Beach Pier into a military installation. Machine guns were positioned at the end of the pier, serving as a defensive measure against potential enemy threats that might approach from the sea. The pier, which was a popular gathering spot for locals and visitors, now played a crucial role in safeguarding the coastline.

Another interesting development was the conversion of a local elementary school's basement into a military communications center. Today known as Dwyer Middle School, this educational institution became an integral part of the military's efforts. The basement of the school provided a secure and central location for coordinating communications during the war. This transformation highlighted the city's commitment to supporting the war effort and utilizing every available resource to ensure the safety and security of the nation.

The military presence in Huntington Beach extended beyond these specific locations. The local beaches and coastline were closely monitored and patrolled by military personnel. Soldiers were stationed along the shores, keeping a watchful eye for any signs of enemy activity. The city's residents appreciated the heightened security measures, as they provided a sense of safety and reassurance during a time of great uncertainty.

According to historical reports and accounts, the locals generally welcomed the military presence in Huntington Beach. The soldiers became a familiar sight in the community, and their presence instilled a sense of security among the residents. The military personnel often interacted with the locals, forging friendships and community bonds that lasted beyond the war years. The soldiers' dedication to protecting the city and their willingness to sacrifice for the greater good earned them respect and admiration from the community.

In 1949, the majority of the land was given back to the original gun club owners by the military. Today, you can still see remnants the Panama gun mounts on the lower shelf of the bluff, just below where the gun club once sat. But what was it like after the military left? Was it even possible for the Bolsa Chica Gun Club to return to its former days of grandeur?

18

THE TRANSFORMATION OF THE BOLSA CHICA GUN CLUB

U pon the return of the property to the gun club owners, the club had to invest a significant amount of money into renovating the facility. The presence of the military and the subsequent removal of the artillery guns caused damage or alterations to the existing infrastructure, which needed to be repaired or restored.

After the renovations, the gun club resumed its operations for a brief period. However, interest in the facility and the hunting reserve began to decline. There were various reasons for this decline. Firstly, the ecological balance of the wetlands had been greatly disturbed by the presence of oil production activities. This disruption had negatively impacted the local wildlife, including duck populations, making hunting less fruitful and less appealing to enthusiasts.

Additionally, the surrounding area experienced significant development, which encroached upon the gun club's premises. This urbanization made it less safe and less practical to continue operating a gun club in that location. As a result, the gun club made a transition and transformed into a restaurant and social facility, catering to a different clientele and offering new types of recreational activities.

As well, as Orange County underwent rapid development in the postwar era, the demand for recreational shooting decreased due to the urbanization of the surrounding areas. This shift in demographics and cultural preferences prompted the Bolsa Chica Gun Club to reevaluate its purpose and appeal to a wider audience. Recognizing the need for change, the club decided to embrace its picturesque location and transform into a social club.

Throughout the late 1940s and 1950s, the club began catering to a diverse range of events, including cocktail parties at sunset. The breathtaking views offered by the club's location, with its vast green lawns and scenic surroundings, made it an ideal setting for social gatherings. Members and guests could relax and enjoy the natural beauty while socializing and indulging in cocktails, fostering a vibrant social atmosphere.

Additionally, the club hosted weddings, capitalizing on its charming ambiance and unique setting. Couples seeking a memorable and picturesque location for their special day found the Bolsa Chica Gun Club to be an ideal choice. The club's open spaces, manicured lawns and stunning sunsets provided a romantic backdrop for these joyous celebrations.

In the mid-1950s, recognizing the need to further diversify its offerings, the Bolsa Chica Gun Club's restaurant became open to the public. This move not only expanded the club's revenue streams but also solidified its reputation as a social hub. The restaurant capitalized on the club's scenic location, offering patrons an opportunity to enjoy a delicious meal while overlooking the emerald green lawns and picturesque vistas.

The club's restaurant quickly became a popular dining destination, attracting visitors from both within and outside of Orange County. Patrons relished the opportunity to savor delectable cuisine in a unique and tranquil setting far removed from the hustle and bustle of urban life. The restaurant catered to both club members and the broader public, further cementing the club's reputation as a premier social destination.

Thomas Talbert, the grandson of pioneer Tom Talbert, shared his thoughts on his experiences at the Bolsa Chica Gun Club not long before he passed away in February 2023. He was born in 1938, prior to World War II. He shared:

The circumstances that led to my visit were quite interesting. At that time, Thomas's uncle and his wife were working as caretakers of the gun club. They lived on the premises in a small house, which became my gateway to a world of excitement and adventure. Although hunting activities had started to dwindle due to the growing development of neighboring communities, there was still an aura of charm and history surrounding the club.

I distinctly remember the times when I would visit the club, usually on weekends when my relatives had a little more free time to spend with me. As a young boy, those moments were filled with wonder and anticipation. The gun club, with its rustic appeal and natural surroundings, was a fascinating place for a child like me. I would explore every nook and cranny, soaking in the atmosphere.

He added, "The once-thriving hunting grounds slowly gave way to the encroachment of nearby communities. The sounds of guns and the thrill of the hunt were gradually replaced by the sounds of construction and the birth of new neighborhoods."

Nevertheless, those visits to the Bolsa Chica Gun Club left an indelible mark on his young mind. The camaraderie Thomas experienced with his relatives, the joy of discovering hidden corners of the club and the fading echoes of a bygone era all contributed to the enchantment he felt during those weekends.

They even went a step further in fostering his love for the outdoors and hunting. Thomas's relatives, recognizing his enthusiasm, gifted him his very own .22-caliber rifle. It was a prized possession, and with their guidance and supervision, he had the opportunity to go out shooting jack rabbits on the club's expansive property. Those moments of aiming, firing and experiencing the thrill of the hunt were etched in his memory forever.

One particular aspect of the club that left a lasting impression on him was the grandeur of the main dining area. To his young eyes, it appeared massive and palatial, exuding an air of elegance and sophistication. His relatives explained to him that this was where wealthy individuals would retreat for a day, seeking solace and leisure. Although, by that time, the club had transformed into more of a social hub, the echoes of its prestigious past were still palpable.

As young Thomas wandered through the club's grounds, he observed men engaged in various recreational activities. Some were skillfully putting

The Bolsa Chica Gun Club featured a modern kitchen in the 1930s. *Author's collection.*

golf balls on well-manicured greens, while others enjoyed the timeless game of horseshoes. The atmosphere was alive with friendly competition and the camaraderie that comes from shared interests. It was a place where people gathered to unwind, forge connections and revel in the simple pleasures of life.

In those moments, he witnessed the club as a microcosm of a bygone era, where a sense of community and a love for the outdoors intertwined seamlessly. The sight of individuals engaging in leisurely pursuits against the backdrop of the changing landscape served as a poignant reminder of the passage of time and the evolving nature of our surroundings.

As time passed, life took its course, and the memories of the Bolsa Chica Gun Club became cherished treasures of the past. Thomas was grateful to have had the opportunity to hear his stories and be transported back to a time when hunting and nature intertwined with family connections.

Thomas Talbert's recollections of the gun club serve as a reminder of the ever-changing landscape and the importance of preserving our history and heritage. The Bolsa Chica Gun Club may have faded away, but its memory lives on through the stories and experiences shared by those who were fortunate enough to witness its glory days. The Bolsa Chica Gun Club may have been just one chapter in a much larger story, but it held a special place in Talbert's heart as a testament to the bond between family, nature and the passage of time.

Diane Deal Tollefson remembers the club as well. She recounted what it was like to have lunch there.

When I was a young girl, around 1952, I had the most unforgettable experience at the Bolsa Chica Gun Club. I must have been about ten years old at the time. It was a sunny day, and I remember sitting at a window table on the northern side of the club, overlooking the magnificent ocean. The moment I stepped inside, it reminded me of going to Bullock's department store in downtown Los Angeles. The gun club had a restaurant that felt like a place for wealthy people. It exuded elegance with its linen napkins, tablecloth, beautiful restaurant china, and glistening silverware. Although we weren't members, the restaurant was open to the public. I think I ordered a simple tuna sandwich, and to my surprise, it was absolutely delicious. It felt like a treat, eating such a scrumptious meal in such a distinguished setting. The interior of the club had a grand atmosphere, adorned with large pictures hanging on the walls. I couldn't help but feel a sense of awe and sophistication being there. One of our family friends, who was familiar with the area, brought my mother and me to the gun club. She worked nearby and suggested that we stop there on our way back home to the Los Angeles area from San Diego. It was open to the public at that time. I'm grateful she did because it turned out to be a truly special experience.

In addition to its transformation into a social club and restaurant, the Bolsa Chica Gun Club embraced its expansive green lawns and scenic surroundings by hosting dog shows, with a particular focus on cocker spaniels. The club's vast, meticulously maintained lawns provided an ideal venue for showcasing these elegant dogs and their impressive skills. The popularity of these dog shows further enhanced the club's reputation and drew in crowds from near and far.

The club also occasionally hosted other special events, such as croquet tournaments and horseshoe tossing competitions. These activities, combined with the serene atmosphere and beautiful surroundings, offered members and visitors a unique and enjoyable recreational experience.

The transformation of the Bolsa Chica Gun Club into a social club and event venue reflected the changing times and the evolving needs of the community. As the development of Orange County limited the viability of traditional gun clubs, the Bolsa Chica Gun Club adapted to remain relevant and appealing.

By embracing its stunning location, the club capitalized on its natural beauty and scenic vistas. The introduction of social gatherings, weddings and a public restaurant transformed the club into a vibrant social hub. Members and guests could enjoy cocktails at sunset, celebrate special occasions and indulge in fine dining while basking in the club's picturesque surroundings. But things were changing even more at the Bolsa Chica Gun Club by this point, including who could claim ownership.

19

OWNERSHIP

B y the 1950s, the ownership structure of Bolsa Chica had also changed significantly. Instead of the original gun club members, there were now over two hundred owners in control of the Bolsa Chica property. These owners consisted of a small number of original gun club members who remained involved and the heirs of deceased members who had inherited their shares.

This complex ownership structure posed challenges when it came to approving new drilling leases or implementing other actions that affected the collective owners. The oil company involved in the drilling operations would often complain about the difficulties of dealing with over two hundred landowners and their respective attorneys. The multitude of owners and the associated legal representation made the decision-making process more cumbersome and time-consuming.

However, despite the challenges, the collective owners and their heirs retained the surface rights of Bolsa Chica until 1970. At this point, they made the decision to sell their interests. The surface rights of Bolsa Chica were sold for a substantial sum of $28,620,000 to a land development subsidiary of Signal Oil and Gas called Signal Landmark.

The sale of the surface rights to Signal Landmark marked a significant turning point in the history of Bolsa Chica. It signaled a shift from the previous gun club and hunting reserve use to a new phase focused on land development. The involvement of Signal Landmark suggested an intention to explore and exploit the property's potential for non-oil-related development, potentially transforming the area in line with their land development expertise and objectives.

After the war, the Bolsa Chica area remained under the ownership of the Bolsa Land Corporation, which was made up of approximately three hundred individuals who were either members of the Bolsa Chica Gun Club or their descendants. The gun club members still engaged in hunting activities near the clubhouse, particularly at the duck pond located southeast of it. The area continued to attract a significant number of ducks.

However, the presence of non-members who constructed blinds using debris and palm fronds on the beach to shoot the birds as they flew from the ocean toward the ponds became a source of frustration for the gun club members. These unauthorized hunting activities interfered with the club's operations and disturbed its members.

Local children often ventured onto the property to explore and search for rabbits. This added to the club's concerns about trespassing and the potential disruption of their recreational activities.

In the 1950s, the government implemented a flood control channel in Bolsa Chica, which had already undergone changes by the gun club members. This government intervention further altered the landscape and ecosystem of Bolsa Chica. The construction of the flood control channel resulted in the separation of the lower wetlands from the upper mesa. Additionally, the channel introduced urban runoff into what was once a pristine area.

The flood control channel was constructed to manage and divert excess water during periods of heavy rainfall and prevent flooding in nearby urban areas. However, this engineering intervention had unintended consequences for the natural environment of Bolsa Chica.

By physically separating the lower wetlands from the upper mesa, the flood control channel disrupted the natural hydrology of the area. This separation hindered the normal flow of water, affecting the movement of sediment, nutrients and organisms throughout the ecosystem. Consequently, it altered the natural processes that supported the diverse plant and animal communities in Bolsa Chica.

As well, the introduction of urban runoff into the previously untouched area had a negative impact on water quality. Urban runoff often carries pollutants, such as chemicals, fertilizers and sediment from roads, buildings and other human activities. These pollutants can be harmful to aquatic life and can degrade the overall ecological health of the wetlands.

It's important to note that the construction of the flood control channel was likely aimed at addressing human needs for flood protection and urban

An aerial shot of the gun club property, circa the late 1930s. *Author's collection.*

development. However, such interventions often have unintended ecological consequences. Over the years, there has been increased recognition of the importance of preserving and restoring wetland ecosystems, and efforts have been made to mitigate the impacts of past alterations in places like Bolsa Chica.

In 1950, the gun club received an exemption from paying state franchise taxes under section 23701G of the revenue and taxation code. This particular provision allowed for an exemption for recreational clubs like the gun club. This exemption provided some financial relief to the gun club members and supported the continued operation of the club during that time.

The Bolsa Land Company, which owned the property, aimed to develop it into a small craft harbor and marina, along with residential development.

To facilitate their plans, the Bolsa Land Company reorganized into several individual corporations, each named after the specific areas of anticipated development. These corporations included Bolsa Grande, Bolsa Huntington, Bolsa Laguna, Bolsa Los Patos and Bolsa Mesa.

However, the development plans faced significant opposition from local activists and environmental concerns. As a result, the proposed development

Buildings Cleared off Beach Gun Club Land

HUNTINGTON BEACH —Bulldozers have reduced to kindling wood most of the buildings at Bolsa Chica Gun Club, whose marshy lands once yielded bountiful harvests of mallard ducks and black gold.

William Gallienne, Chamber of Commerce manager, said furnishings also have been removed from buildings at the club which occupies 2,000 acres of land north of Coast Highway near here.

Five men who liked duck hunting, but who probably knew very little about oil, formed the Bolsa Land Co. in 1899, according to Gallienne.

Thirty shares of stock, at $1,000 each, were issued to

In 1921 oil began spouting up through blackberry patches in Huntington Beach and Standard Oil Co. leased the gun club tract for 20 years.

Probably no club outside of Las Vegas or Monte Carlo ever had such riches as did this duck club.

For example, in the year of 1942 the club's income was an estimated $1.5 million.

War Tax Bills

About that time, Gallienne recalls, war tax bills were threatening to cut deeply into excess profits and the property was sliced into 108 pieces to represent respective interests of the share-

Left: The news of the 1964 gun club razing. *From the* Los Angeles Times.

Below: The gun club location, circa 1970. The main buildings are gone, but some of the support structures remained at that time. All are gone today. *Author's collection.*

In the 1970s, some of the support structures were still standing. Today, they are all gone. *Author's collection.*

did not come to fruition. The gun club, which was a part of the Bolsa Chica area, disbanded in January 1964, and the clubhouse was subsequently demolished in July 1964.

In the 1960s, Signal Landmark, a real estate company, acquired the two thousand acres of the Bolsa Chica Wetlands. They had plans to develop a large-scale housing project and marina in the area. However, the proposed development faced objections from some state officials and concerned individuals.

In 1970, the Bolsa Chica facility was purchased by the Signal Oil and Gas Company from the Bolsa Corporations, all of which had originated from the original Bolsa Land Company. Signal then transferred the property's title to its holding subsidiary, the Signal Land and Development Company. The Bolsa Chica Gun Club continued its operations under Signal Oil and Gas ownership until it eventually disbanded.

In 1973, as a compromise, the developer agreed to set aside three hundred acres of wetlands along Pacific Coast Highway for preservation. These preserved wetlands became the original Bolsa Chica Ecological Reserve. The establishment of this reserve marked an important step in recognizing the ecological value of the wetlands and preserving a portion of the natural habitat.

In 1976, members of the League of Women Voters were dissatisfied with the relatively small amount of wetlands being preserved and formed a new group called the Amigos de Bolsa Chica. The purpose of this group was to advocate for the protection and preservation of more of the Bolsa Chica Wetlands.

Then in 1992, the Bolsa Chica Land Trust was established. The land trust aimed to preserve not only the lower wetlands but the entire Bolsa Chica area. Its goal was to protect and restore the wetlands, as well as conserve the surrounding uplands and other habitats within Bolsa Chica.

These grassroots efforts by concerned individuals and organizations played a crucial role in raising awareness about the importance of preserving the Bolsa Chica Wetlands. Their actions contributed to the establishment of the Bolsa Chica Ecological Reserve and the broader preservation efforts undertaken by the Bolsa Chica Land Trust. These initiatives have helped protect and restore the wetlands, ensuring the conservation of this valuable ecological area. For all the mythical members and guests that once roamed the area, there was still one colorful character left to leave his mark.

20

"SMOKY" STEVENS

fter the Bolsa Chica Gun Club was razed in 1964, Alvin Stevens,
known by his nickname "Smoky," took over a small cottage on the bluff
along with his wife, Myrtle; their three border collies; and about two
dozen Nubian goats as well as some chickens. This cottage was located in
the vicinity of the marshlands. Smoky, dressed in cowboy attire consisting of
cowboy boots, flannel shirts, Levi's jeans and a cowboy hat, became a local
legend in the Huntington Beach area.

As the caretaker, Smoky was initially hired by the Bolsa Corporation in the
early 1960s and later by its successor, Signal Bolsa Corporation. He took on
the responsibility of maintaining and patrolling the property, behaving much
like a frontier sheriff. He performed his duties with dedication, often driving
around the marshlands in his bright yellow pickup truck accompanied by
his most loyal border collie named Chinquita, who would run ahead as if
serving as a shotgun rider.

Smoky's reputation as the watch guard of the old Bolsa Chica Gun Club
property became legendary within the community of Huntington Beach.
Whether it was equestrians or surfers using the property as a shortcut
to the beach and beyond, everyone was aware of Smoky's presence. His
reputation for wielding a shotgun and firing at trespassers added an air of
excitement and caution to those who ventured near the property. It was an
era characterized by vast open spaces and a rural atmosphere, blending
elements of both a small town and the Old West.

Robin Magness was a young teenager when she and her horse were hit by the rock salt fired by Smoky. While there were rumors that he would brandish a shotgun and shoot indiscriminately, Robin didn't believe it until one day Smoky actually opened fire on her and her horse. Robin was struck on her leg, resulting in a stinging sensation, and her horse became frightened and went into a frenzy while she desperately held on. Despite the incident, she didn't dwell on it as a negative experience. Instead, she viewed it as part of the charm of the area during that time.

In 1974, after a decade of service, Smoky decided to retire from his role as caretaker. However, he continued to reside on the property until 1977, when his cottage was eventually torn down. At that point, he made a significant life change, purchasing five acres of desert land in 29 Palms. He sold his goats, bid farewell to Huntington Beach and relocated to the desert.

Unfortunately, Smoky's departure from Bolsa Chica was followed by tragedy. Just ten days after leaving, on May 7, 1977, Alvin Stevens passed away at the age of seventy-one. His legacy as Smoky Stephens, the caretaker of the wetlands and a local legend in Huntington Beach, remained etched in the memories of those who knew of him.

Smoky Stephens's departure marked the end of an era, both for him personally and for the Bolsa Chica Wetlands. His dedication to protecting the property and his distinctive presence will always be remembered as part of the rich history of the area.

Throughout the late 1970s and through the 1980s, Fred and Alexis Burkett operated Smokey's Stables, which were located on the property of the Bolsa Chica Gun Club. The stables were a popular destination for local children's birthday parties and a place where horse owners could keep their horses. Smokey's Stables owed its name of course to Alvin "Smoky" Stevens.

The stables provided a safe and nurturing environment for horses. Fred and Alexis Burkett were known for their extensive knowledge and experience in horse care, and they ensured that the horses under their care received proper attention, grooming and feeding. They also offered riding lessons and training services for those interested in improving their equestrian skills.

Besides catering to horse owners, Smoky's Stables became a popular venue for children's birthday parties. The spacious grounds and the presence of horses made it an exciting and unique location for celebrations. Children could interact with the horses, ride them under supervision and learn about horse care.

However, in 1989, the Metropolitan Water District, which owned the land where Smoky's Stables were situated, terminated the lease. As a result, part

Fred Burkett near the end of his days running Smoky's Stables. *Author's collection.*

of the land was developed into residential homes, and the stables were forced to close down. This decision marked the end of an era for Smokey's Stables and the horse community that had enjoyed its services for many years.

Despite the closure of Smoky's Stables, the memories of the Burkett family's dedication to horse care and their contribution to the local community live on. The stable's legacy is intertwined with the fond memories of children's birthday parties, the joy of horse owners and the recognition of the legendary caretaker Smoky Stevens. And even though they were gone, the famed World War II bunkers remained. How did those factor into a more modern society?

BUNKERS IN THE MODERN AGE

During the 1970s into the early 1990s, the underground World War II bunkers provided a secluded and thrilling environment for young people to engage in activities like carousing, drinking beer, smoking cigarettes and simply exploring the mysterious underground tunnels. The allure of

World War II bunker complex on the gun club property before it was destroyed in the early 1990s. *Author's collection.*

The demolition of one of the large World War II bunkers on the gun club property in the early 1990s. *Author's collection.*

What one of the largest World War II bunkers on the gun club property looked like before it was demolished in the early 1990s. *Author's collection.*

the hidden and forgotten spaces beneath the surface drew many curious teenagers who sought a sense of adventure and a break from the monotony of everyday life.

However, as the 1990s progressed, the city authorities began to address safety concerns associated with the underground bunkers. Additionally, developers had plans to build a series of new homes in the area, necessitating the alteration of the existing landscape. Consequently, the city decided to seal off and fill in some of the bunkers.

These measures were taken both for safety reasons, as the underground tunnels presented potential hazards and risks, and to accommodate the upcoming residential development. The bunkers, once a source of excitement and exploration for teenagers, were now seen as liabilities and obstacles to progress.

By the early 2000s, all the bunkers had been sealed off, closing the chapter on this era of underground exploration. The property was transformed to suit the needs of the new housing development, and the hidden tunnels were no longer accessible to the public.

Today, the Bolsa Chica Gun Club and its underground bunkers stand as a relic of a bygone era, remembered by those who experienced the thrill of exploring its hidden depths during the 1980s and 1990s. The sealing off of the bunkers marked the end of an era, but the memories of teenage adventure and the mystique of the underground tunnels still linger in the minds of those who partook in those escapades. However, for one man, there was still more to be uncovered.

21

A SURVEY AND THEN A WIN
FOR THE FARMERS

I n the early 1990s, a veil of curiosity descended on the sprawling wetlands
of Bolsa Chica as Doug McIntosh embarked on a remarkable journey.
Armed with his systematic pedestrian archaeological survey, he ventured
deep into the heart of the Bolsa Chica Gun Club site, unraveling untold
secrets of its industrial archaeology. What lay beneath the surface was a
tapestry of history waiting to be unveiled.

As the survey unfolded, McIntosh's diligent crew meticulously traversed
the wetlands, their eyes attuned to the whispers of the past. Their efforts
were not in vain, for they discovered a treasure trove of knowledge. It was
not solely the remnants of a forgotten era that they stumbled upon; it was a
window into an intricate web of stories waiting to be told.

With every step, they unearthed prehistoric artifacts, the relics of a time
long gone. Each piece spoke volumes, whispering tales of ancient civilizations
that once thrived on this land. But their endeavor was not limited to mere
documentation. Armed with their lenses and sketchbooks, they captured the
very essence of the forgotten past. Photographs immortalized the remnants,
while maps guided their way through the labyrinthine wetlands, weaving a
tangible connection between past and present.

Yet as they delved deeper into the secrets of Bolsa Chica, an astonishing
revelation awaited them. Amid the faint ruins of the gun club structures,
their keen eyes discerned the forgotten souls of wooden water diversion
features. These age-worn conduits, weathered by the relentless passage of
time, had guided the ebb and flow of water, orchestrating a silent dance with

An early 1990s survey photograph of the club property. *Courtesy of Doug McIntosh.*

nature itself. They were silent witnesses to a century of change, their silent whispers echoing through the marshes.

But the story did not end there. McIntosh's discerning gaze fell on the proud figure of a Byron Jackson pump, standing stoically against the backdrop of the wetlands. A mechanical marvel of its time, this pump had labored tirelessly, its rhythmic heartbeat once reverberating through the air. It was a testament to man's relentless pursuit of progress, a symbol of the interplay between industry and nature.

And then, amid the vast expanse, they discovered the original wooden hunting blinds, stoically perched as guardians of a forgotten era. These humble structures, once witnesses to exhilarating chases and triumphant victories, now stood as silent sentinels of history. They whispered tales of camaraderie and the thrill of the hunt, bridging the gap between man and nature in a way only hunters can comprehend.

But the tale took an unexpected twist, as if the very fabric of time had woven a connection between past and present. McIntosh's ancestry intertwined with the narrative, revealing a poignant link to the land he stood on. In the 1930s, his great-grandfather J.W. McIntosh leased the very same site for cattle grazing. It seemed as though fate had conspired to bring the family's story full circle, binding their legacy to this hallowed ground. In the

An early 1990s survey photograph of the club property. *Courtesy of Doug McIntosh.*

end, McIntosh's systematic survey transcended the superficial boundaries of historical research. It breathed life into forgotten structures and artifacts, stitching them together into a vibrant tapestry of human endeavor and untamed wilderness. Through McIntosh's meticulous efforts, the industrial archaeology of the Bolsa Chica Gun Club property found its rightful place in the annals of history, no longer overshadowed by the usual focus on just buildings and people.

McIntosh's survey unearthed a hidden narrative that had long been overlooked by historians. No longer would the focus rest solely on the gun club building, for the wooden water diversion features, the Byron Jackson pumps and the hunting blinds emerged as vital characters in the tale. They provided a complete and vivid account of the property's rich history, offering a glimpse into the lives and endeavors of those who had come before.

The story of Bolsa Chica Gun Club was no longer confined to the pages of textbooks or the fading memories of those who once frequented its halls. McIntosh's survey had breathed new life into the forgotten corners of the wetlands, resurrecting the spirits of the past.

As McIntosh walked the land his great-grandfather had once grazed his cattle on, he couldn't help but feel a profound connection. It was as if the echoes of the past reverberated through his veins, reminding him of the enduring legacy that tied him to this very place. His journey had not only uncovered the secrets of the Bolsa Chica Gun Club but also rekindled a personal bond that transcended time.

The systematic pedestrian archaeological survey had left an indelible mark, not only on the wetlands but also on the hearts and minds of those who followed the footsteps of Doug McIntosh. The story of the Bolsa Chica Gun Club would forever be remembered as a vibrant tapestry woven from the threads of history, brought to life by the relentless pursuit of knowledge and the passion for unearthing hidden stories.

And as the winds whispered through the marshes, carrying the echoes of the past, McIntosh knew that the spirit of Bolsa Chica would continue to captivate future generations. Its industrial archaeology, once hidden beneath layers of time, had been laid bare, inviting all who ventured there to listen, learn and appreciate the profound beauty that lies within the untold stories of our collective heritage. The ghosts were all fading at the site of the Bolsa Chica Gun Club. By now, more than one hundred years had passed since the farmers first put up their fight to keep the waterways open in the area. Could it be that vindication was now suddenly possible?

In August 2006, the community of Huntington Beach and the surrounding areas were buzzing with excitement and anticipation as the long-awaited reopening of the tidal inlet at Bolsa Chica approached. The prospect of ocean water flowing freely into the wetlands after more than a century was met with overwhelming joy and a sense of triumph over a past environmental mistake.

The local residents had witnessed the slow degradation of the Bolsa Chica Wetlands over the years, and many were aware of the history behind the gun club's decision to seal off the water to create a freshwater hunting environment. It was widely recognized as a selfish act that had led to a severe decline in biodiversity and the loss of a once-thriving ecosystem.

As news of the impending reopening spread, the community came together in anticipation. There was a palpable sense of hope and optimism as people recognized the potential for a remarkable environmental restoration. The thought of witnessing the wetlands once again brimming with life, teeming with diverse marine species and serving as a sanctuary for migratory birds was incredibly exciting.

Community organizations, environmentalists and nature enthusiasts collaborated to spread the word and educate others about the significance of this event. They held public meetings, organized educational programs and conducted awareness campaigns to rally support for the reopening of the tidal inlet. The shared enthusiasm was contagious, and the community united in a collective effort to give the wetlands a chance to heal and thrive once more.

When the day finally arrived and the tidal inlet was reopened, the excitement was palpable. People gathered along the shores, eagerly awaiting the moment when the ocean waters would rush in, signaling a new era for Bolsa Chica. Cheers erupted as the first waves made their way through the channel, carrying with them the promise of rejuvenation and restoration.

Witnessing the transformation unfold was a sight to behold. The wetlands, which had long been starved of the life-giving force of the ocean, gradually began to heal. Native plants and vegetation quickly took root, providing habitats for countless species of birds, fish and other wildlife. The return of vibrant marshes, brackish water and tidal influence brought back the natural balance and ecological diversity that had been absent for so long.

The community of Huntington Beach and the surrounding areas celebrated this milestone as a triumph for environmental conservation and a testament to the power of collective action. It was a moment of pride and joy, as the community had played an indispensable role in correcting a terrible mistake from the past and allowing nature to reclaim its rightful place.

The reopening of the tidal inlet at Bolsa Chica became a symbol of hope and inspiration for communities worldwide. It served as a reminder that even in the face of past environmental errors, it is never too late to rectify them and restore the delicate balance of nature. The excitement and pride felt by the community in 2006 were a testament to the enduring spirit of environmental stewardship and the belief in a brighter, sustainable future.

As the water flowed freely once again, the wetlands began to rejuvenate. Marine life returned, bird populations soared and the area became a haven for environmental enthusiasts and nature lovers. The transformation was nothing short of miraculous, and the people of Bolsa Chica couldn't help but feel a sense of poetic justice.

Some believed that on that day in 2006, the spirits of the local farmers who had suffered the consequences of the gun club's actions were smiling. The environmental chaos caused by the wealthy and powerful members of the club had come full circle, and nature had reclaimed its rightful place. It served as a reminder that the actions we take today can have far-reaching consequences and that, ultimately, the balance of nature cannot be easily disrupted or controlled. Despite how much has changed over the years, you can still pick up faint traces at the site.

22

A WALK TODAY

Walking the trails at the Bolsa Chica wetlands today is nothing short of a magical experience. As you meander through the picturesque landscape, a sense of wonder and curiosity fills the air. Amid the natural beauty lies a hidden treasure—a glimpse into the remnants of the past, specifically the Bolsa Chica Gun Club. Though not abundant, these compelling fragments hold a profound allure for those who know where to look.

As you traverse the trails, your eyes are drawn to small but captivating traces of the past. Bits of curbing and sidewalk, weathered by time, once led visitors to the famed cedar and redwood lodge. These humble remnants serve as silent witnesses to the lively gatherings and joyous occasions that once graced this historic venue.

The landscape itself whispers tales of the past. Towering palm trees and majestic eucalyptus trees, brought in over a century ago to enhance the property's aesthetics, still proudly stand. Their presence evokes a sense of timelessness, connecting the present-day wanderer to those who trod these very paths long ago.

Beyond the protective fence that encloses the primary area, further secrets await. Random bits of fencing, once strong and sturdy, now bear the patina of age and the marks of weathering. Their dilapidated state hints at the passage of time and the stories they could tell if only they could speak.

Opposite, top: An information panel at the site details some of the gun club's history. *Photograph by Tamara Asaki.*

Opposite, bottom: An information panel at the site details some of the gun club's history. *Photograph by Tamara Asaki.*

Above: Some of the remnants that remain on the other side of the fence at the site of the Bolsa Chica Gun Club. *Author's collection.*

The palm trees now mark the former site of the Bolsa Chica Gun Club. *Photograph by Tamara Asaki.*

One of the two World War II Panama gun mounts still visible near the former site of the Bolsa Chica Gun Club. *Photograph by Tamara Asaki.*

Rusted farm equipment, long forgotten in the annals of agricultural history, captures the imagination. These silent sentinels, once vital to the daily workings of the land, now rest in peaceful abandonment. Their mere presence conjures images of toil and sweat, painting a vivid picture of a bygone era. Old corral pens, their timeworn wooden slats standing as a testament to the past, complete the tableau. These pens, once bustling with the comings and goings of livestock, now stand empty, their purpose fulfilled. Yet their empty spaces seem to echo with the sounds of lowing cattle and the shouts of cowboys.

In the quiet solitude of the wetlands, there is an undeniable resonance—a haunting beauty that lingers in the imagination. Each remnant, each artifact, invites the observer to step back in time and envision the vibrant scenes that unfolded in this very place. The mind conjures images of lively conversations, laughter and the clinking of glasses, intermingled with the sounds of nature. To walk the trails at the Bolsa Chica Wetlands today is to embark on a journey of discovery and reflection. It is to be transported to a different era, where the past intertwines with the present and the whispers of history echo through the windswept grasses. It is a reminder that the land we tread on carries the weight of countless stories, waiting to be unveiled by those who seek them.

In this magical experience, the Bolsa Chica Wetlands unveil their secrets to those who are willing to listen—to those who know where to look. And in the quiet contemplation of these remnants, one can't help but feel a deep connection to the generations who came before and a profound appreciation for the enduring beauty of this remarkable place.

23

IS ANYTHING LEFT?

While the physical remnants of the Bolsa Chica Gun Club may be scarce, the stories and artifacts that have survived continue to captivate the imaginations of those interested in the history of Huntington Beach. These fragments serve as a reminder of the vibrant past of the gun club and its place in the community's collective memory.

Virgil Brewster's journey to owning Brewster's Ice, a family-owned icehouse in downtown Huntington Beach, is a fascinating tale of resilience, ingenuity and a deep connection to the local community. It all began during World War II, when the Bolsa Chica Gun Club, located in Huntington Beach, was transformed into a military barracks and a structure on the premises served as a meat locker for soldiers.

Virgil Brewster, a driven and ambitious entrepreneur, recognized the potential in repurposing this structure and transforming it into something valuable for the community. With a keen eye for business opportunities, he saw the demand for ice during those war years and envisioned a thriving icehouse that could cater to the needs of both residents and businesses.

Undeterred by the challenges ahead, Brewster negotiated with the authorities and managed to acquire the structure that had been used as a meat locker. He arranged for it to be transported from the Bolsa Chica Gun Club location to downtown Huntington Beach, where it stands today as Brewster's Ice. This relocation was no small feat and required careful planning, logistics and the support of a dedicated team.

Once the structure was successfully moved, Brewster wasted no time in converting it into an icehouse. He installed state-of-the-art ice-making equipment, ensuring a reliable supply of ice to meet the demands of the community. The icehouse quickly gained a reputation for its high-quality ice and exceptional service, becoming a go-to destination for local residents and businesses alike.

Today, Brewster's Ice still stands proudly just off Main and Sixth Streets, a testament to the entrepreneurial spirit of Virgil Brewster and the enduring legacy of his family. It remains a treasured establishment, providing ice to local residents, restaurants and businesses while also serving as a symbol of the rich history and strong sense of community in Huntington Beach.

As for the actual gun club, of course very little remains today. During World War II, when the army took over the facility, many of the original detail pieces, including furniture and the iconic chandeliers, were auctioned off, resulting in the loss of much of the club's original character and charm.

However, amid the scattered remnants of the gun club's history, there is one known item that has survived the test of time—a tobacco table. This table, which was located within the gun club, found its way into the possession

Brewster's Ice House as it looks today in downtown Huntington Beach. *Author's collection.*

The tobacco desk from the Bolsa Chica Gun Club. *Author's collection.*

of a Huntington Beach local named Meredith Tsunehara. Her grandfather, who served as the caretaker for Hampton Story, who was one of the original charter members of the gun club, gifted her the table many years ago.

The tobacco table holds significant sentimental value for Meredith and her family, as it serves as a tangible link to the history and legacy of the Bolsa Chica Gun Club. Its presence is a reminder of the bygone era when the gun club thrived, attracting members and visitors who enjoyed its offerings and camaraderie.

During the filming of a television episode about the gun club, Meredith reached out and agreed to be interviewed for the program by this author; she shared her family's connection to the gun club and the significance of the table. In an incredible act of trust, Meredith decided to entrust the desk to the this author for safekeeping.

The tobacco table itself is a beautifully crafted piece, showcasing intricate design details that reflect the craftsmanship of its time. Its presence evokes a sense of nostalgia and curiosity, inviting individuals to imagine the conversations and gatherings that took place around it during the gun club's heyday.

Detail of the tobacco desk from the Bolsa Chica Gun Club. *Author's collection.*

In addition to the tobacco table, another intriguing relic associated with the Bolsa Chica Gun Club is an original "No Trespassing" sign. This sign, which belonged to the renowned Robert "The Greek" Bolen, a legendary surfboard shaper and designer who has been an integral part of Huntington Beach history since the 1950s, represents a connection to the past and the enduring spirit of the local surf culture.

The original 1910 Bolsa Chica gun club map displayed at the Bolsa Chica Conservancy Interpretive Center is a valuable item for understanding the club's layout and operations during that time. The original book of gun club bylaws owned by local writer Luann Murray is a great resource for understanding the rules and regulations governing the club's activities, and it provides valuable insights into the club's culture and practices. The 1919 map and a book from 1898 titled *Wild Fowl of North America*, owned by local historian Darrell Rivers, are also intriguing. The fact that the club's name is handwritten on the back cover of the book suggests a connection between the Bolsa Chica Gun Club and the library it maintained.

Respected Huntington Beach nature photographer Tammy Asaki has developed a unique fascination with the last remaining fragments of the Bolsa Chica Gun Club—the small bits of colored tile that occasionally surface around the former site, particularly after rainfall. While her primary

The author shooting an episode of his television show *Hidden Huntington Beach* at the site of the Bolsa Chica Gun Club. *Author's collection.*

Rare signage from the Bolsa Chica Gun Club. *Author's collection.*

Left: The author holding the "No Trespassing" sign from the Bolsa Chica Gun Club. *Author's collection.*

Below: An original 1910 map of the gun club property. *Author's collection.*

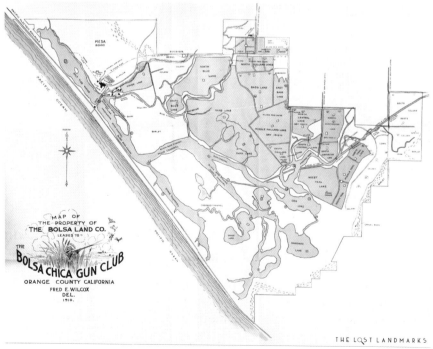

A History

A rare 1919 map of the gun club property. *Author's collection.*

focus is capturing the beauty of birds through her lens, Tammy's love for history draws her to these tantalizing remnants.

As Tammy ventures into the area in search of avian subjects, her keen eye also scans the ground, curious about what relics might be revealed by nature's hand. When the rain washes away the dirt and grime, it unveils glimpses of the past in the form of colorful tiles. These tiles, once part of the vibrant interior of the gun club, now lie scattered and weathered, serving as silent witnesses to the club's rich history.

For Tammy, collecting these tiles has become a personal quest, a way to connect with the heritage of Huntington Beach and pay homage to the bygone era of the gun club. Picking up each fragment, she imagines the grandeur and elegance that once adorned the club's walls and floors. The tiles, with their vibrant hues and intricate patterns, tell stories of gatherings, celebrations and shared moments that have long since faded into memory.

Tammy's love for history intertwines seamlessly with her passion for photography. As she captures the beauty of birds in their natural habitats, she is simultaneously drawn to the remnants of human history that dot the landscape. Through her camera lens, she immortalizes both the living creatures and the fragments of the past, bridging the gap between nature and culture.

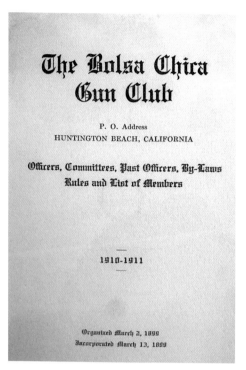

The Bolsa Chica Gun Club

P. O. Address
HUNTINGTON BEACH, CALIFORNIA

Officers, Committees, Past Officers, By-Laws
Rules and List of Members

1910-1911

Organized March 2, 1899
Incorporated March 13, 1899

Left: Original club bylaws. *Author's collection.*

Below, left: The front cover of rare book believed to have been part of the Bolsa Chica Gun Club library. *Courtesy of Darrell Rivers.*

Below, right: The back cover of rare book believed to have been part of the Bolsa Chica Gun Club library. *Courtesy of Darrell Rivers.*

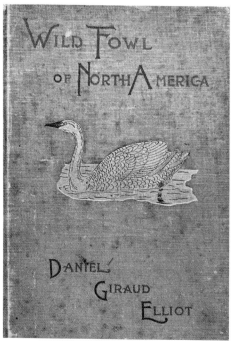

Some of the tiles collected by Tamara Asaki. *Photograph by Tamara Asaki.*

Photographer Tamara Asaki. *Courtesy of Tamara Asaki.*

Some of the tiles and artifacts collected by Tamara Asaki. *Photograph by Tamara Asaki.*

Each tile that Tammy collects becomes a tangible piece of the gun club's legacy. She carefully catalogues them, cherishing their uniqueness and the stories they hold. In her collection, she sees not just tiles but artifacts of a time when the Bolsa Chica Gun Club stood as a vibrant gathering place, echoing with laughter, camaraderie and the clinking of glasses.

Tammy's efforts in preserving these fragments of history serve as a testament to the power of curiosity and the importance of honoring the past. Through her photographs and her collection, she invites others to appreciate the beauty of both the present moment, captured in the flight of birds, and the echoes of history, embodied in the tiles of the Bolsa Chica Gun Club.

In her own unique way, Tammy has become a guardian of the club's memory, allowing its essence to live on through her photographs and the fragments she collects. Her work serves as a gentle reminder that history is not confined to textbooks and museums but can be discovered in unexpected places, waiting to be uncovered by those with an eye for detail and a love for the stories it holds. With that, we can finally address one of the bigger questions that remains.

24

WHO TAKES CARE OF THE AREA TODAY?

The Bolsa Chica Wetlands, encompassing the former property of the Bolsa Chica Gun Club, is a vital ecological site located along the Southern California coast. Today, the wetlands are maintained and protected through the collaborative efforts of three prominent organizations: the Bolsa Chica Conservancy, Amigos de Bolsa Chica and the Bolsa Chica Land Trust.

The Bolsa Chica Conservancy is a nonprofit organization dedicated to the preservation, restoration and education of the Bolsa Chica Wetlands. They play a crucial role in managing the wetlands by engaging in various conservation activities. The conservancy focuses on habitat restoration, water quality improvement and the reintroduction of native plant and animal species. They also organize educational programs, guided tours and community outreach initiatives to raise awareness about the importance of wetland ecosystems and promote their long-term protection.

The aforementioned Amigos de Bolsa Chica is another nonprofit group that actively works toward the preservation and enhancement of the Bolsa Chica Wetlands. Comprising dedicated volunteers, they play an instrumental role in organizing restoration projects, including removing invasive species, planting native vegetation and monitoring wildlife populations. Additionally, Amigos de Bolsa Chica conducts regular clean-up events to maintain the cleanliness and integrity of the wetlands, ensuring a healthy environment for both wildlife and visitors.

A 1964 pen sketch of the Bolsa Chica Gun Club by artist W. Donald Smith. *Author's collection.*

Also, the previously mentioned Bolsa Chica Land Trust is a nonprofit organization committed to the acquisition and protection of land within the Bolsa Chica ecosystem. Through strategic partnerships and fundraising efforts, the land trust has successfully secured and conserved significant portions of land surrounding the wetlands. By acquiring and managing these lands, they create buffer zones that safeguard the wetlands from encroaching development and effectively expand the protected area. The land trust also collaborates with scientific researchers to gather data and implement sustainable management practices that support the long-term ecological health of the wetlands.

Collectively, the Bolsa Chica Conservancy, Amigos de Bolsa Chica and the Bolsa Chica Land Trust form a powerful alliance in the ongoing efforts to maintain and protect the Bolsa Chica Wetlands. Their combined dedication, expertise and community engagement have been instrumental in preserving this valuable coastal habitat. Through habitat restoration, educational programs, community involvement and land preservation initiatives, these organizations ensure the long-term sustainability of the wetlands, allowing future generations to appreciate and benefit from the ecological richness of the Bolsa Chica ecosystem.

WHO ACTUALLY OWNS THE LAND?

After a conversation with Patrick Brenden, the former CEO of the Bolsa Chica Conservancy, I finally found the answer to the burning question that had perplexed so many: Who truly owns the land on which the Bolsa Chica Gun Club sits? The answer, as Patrick explained it to me, was both surprising and enlightening.

In essence, he revealed that the ownership of this land extends far beyond the confines of a single individual or entity. It belongs to all of us, every citizen of California, who holds a stake in its preservation and legacy. The acquisition of the property was made possible through the combined efforts and funding of various government entities.

Today, the title of the entire 1,449-acre ecological reserve, including the area occupied by the Bolsa Chica Gun Club, is held by the State Lands Commission. This commission, in turn, contracts with the Department of Fish and Wildlife to manage the site. It's important to note that the state lands commission's role is primarily that of a custodian, as they hold the title to the property but do not directly manage it on-site.

The Department of Fish and Wildlife, on the other hand, takes on the vital responsibility of being the authoritative presence at the Bolsa Chica Wetlands. They have dedicated personnel, such as wardens, who ensure the enforcement of laws, as well as wildlife experts who diligently monitor and protect the bird population while engaging in various conservation efforts.

It struck me profoundly that this treasured piece of land, with its rich history and ecological significance, is not the property of a select few but rather a shared heritage. As citizens, we are entrusted with the responsibility of advocating for its preservation and cherishing its natural wonders. The Bolsa Chica Gun Club, nestled within this vast ecological reserve, stands as a testament to the collective commitment to conservation and the harmonious coexistence of nature and humanity.

EXACT LOCATION

Last but not least, many people still ask this author: Where exactly was the club if I want to walk the area today? The Bolsa Chica Gun Club was located in the Bolsa Chica Wetlands area near Warner Avenue and Pacific Coast Highway in Huntington Beach, California. To visit the site, you can park at the Bolsa Chica Conservancy Interpretive Center, which is near the

The same palm trees that were brought in around 1900 to landscape the gun club remain. *Author's collection.*

An aerial view of the gun club site today. The trees remain. *Author's collection.*

corner of Warner Avenue and Pacific Coast Highway. From the parking lot, you'll be able to see a cluster of palm trees on the upper mesa, which marks the exact location of the gun club.

To reach the site, cross the bridge that connects to the trailhead from the interpretive center. The walk from there to the site is a gentle one, covering a distance of less than half a mile. Once you arrive, you'll find a small sign that provides some historical information about the gun club. Although the area where the club was situated is fenced off, it is still easily visible from the observation area.

WHAT'S NEXT?

One of my future goals regarding the history of the Bolsa Chica Gun Club would be to conduct an extensive historic survey of the gun club property. This would involve utilizing various archaeological techniques, such as excavation and the use of metal detectors to unearth any remnants or artifacts that might still be present today. It's essential to approach this survey with great sensitivity and respect for the Native American history associated with the area.

By investigating what lies on the other side of the fence today, I hope to shed light on the untold stories and hidden aspects of the gun club's history. Uncovering physical evidence from the past can help provide a more comprehensive understanding of the club's activities, its impact on the local community and its historical significance.

Additionally, I aim to create a documentary about the famed gun club. While there may not be an extensive collection of archival footage available, there are interesting photographic assets that can be utilized. By carefully curating these visual materials and combining them with interviews, expert commentary and re-creations, it would be possible to bring the story of the gun club to life on screen.

Throughout this entire process, my intention is to approach the research and documentation with utmost respect for historical accuracy, cultural sensitivity and ethical considerations. By sharing the story of the Bolsa Chica Gun Club through various mediums, I hope to contribute to a broader understanding of its place in history and its impact on the surrounding community. Of course, remnants and trace elements that remain today will help tell that story's deeper levels.

As I bring this book to a close, I find myself reflecting on the incredible journey we've embarked on together—the exploration of the rich history of the Bolsa Chica Gun Club. It has been an honor and a privilege to delve into the past, unearthing forgotten stories and shedding light on the legacy of this remarkable establishment.

But I would be remiss if I did not express my deepest gratitude to the members of the "Hidden Huntington Beach" Facebook group. Your unwavering interest, engagement and shared love for the history of the gun club have been an invaluable source of inspiration throughout this writing process.

Your passion and dedication have not only fueled my own enthusiasm but also connected me with a community of individuals who genuinely care about preserving the past and honoring the stories of those who came before us. Together, we have formed a bond that transcends time, bridging the gap between the gun club's heyday and the present day.

With every comment and every word of encouragement, you have reminded me of the importance of storytelling and the power it holds to connect us across generations. Your support has been instrumental in bringing this project to fruition, and I am eternally grateful for your unwavering interest and involvement.

As the final pages turn and this chapter draws to a close, please accept my heartfelt thanks for being an essential part of this journey. Your passion for history and your dedication to preserving the legacy of the Bolsa Chica Gun Club have made an indelible impact not only on this book but also on the broader tapestry of our shared heritage.

May the memories we have unearthed and the stories we have shared continue to resonate, inspiring future generations to explore, appreciate and protect the treasures of our collective past.

With deepest appreciation,
Chris Epting

BIBLIOGRAPHY

Baker, Candice. "Bolsa Chica's Long History." *Los Angeles Times*, April 21, 2009.

Carlberg, David. *Bolsa Chica: Its History from Prehistoric Times to the Present.* Huntington Beach, CA: Amigos de Bolsa Chica, 2009.

Greenfield, Rosanne. "The Bolsa Chica Wetlands of Huntington Beach: The Changing Environment, Land Use Patterns, and Cultural Values of Its Inhabitants from 500 A.D. to the Present." Master's thesis, California State University, Fullerton, 1990.

Historicwintersburgblogspot.com.

Huntington Beach and Oral History: A Community History Project of the Oral History Program at California State University, Fullerton. Fullerton: University of California, 1982.

Infotech Research Inc. *An Inventory and Evaluation of Cultural Resources, Bolsa Chica Mesa and Huntington Beach Mesa, Orange County, California.* Los Angeles, CA: Infotech Research Inc., 1989.

Los Angeles Times. "Chronology of the Wetlands." August 2, 1987.

Pacific Coast Archaeological Society. "Gun Club on the Hill." *Pacific Coast Archaeological Society Quarterly* 3, no. 3 (1968): 3–7.

PAR Environmental Services. "Cultural Resources Inventory." 1995.

Talbert, Tom. *My 60 Years in California.* Huntington Beach, CA: Huntington Beach News Press, 1953.

Weikel, Dan. "A New Life for Bolsa Chica." *Los Angeles Times*, October 10, 2004.

Additionally, a variety of articles appearing in the Los Angeles Times *and the* Santa Ana Times *from 1899 to the 1950s served as vital informational resources for this project.*

ABOUT THE AUTHOR

hris Epting is a highly accomplished author and journalist known for his extensive work in documenting the history and culture of Orange County, California. With a diverse range of interests spanning music, sports and local heritage, Epting has established himself as an expert in these fields through his engaging writing and extensive research.

Epting has authored several notable books, earning him recognition and awards for his contributions. *Vanishing Orange County* delves into the disappearing landmarks and cultural treasures of the region, capturing the essence of a changing landscape. *The Rock 'n' Roll History of Orange County* explores the vibrant music scene that emerged from the region, showcasing its impact and influence on the larger musical landscape.

In addition to his rock 'n' roll focus, Epting has also delved into the baseball history of Orange County, chronicling the sport's rich heritage in the area. His book titled *Huntington Beach Then and Now* provides a fascinating glimpse into the evolution of this iconic coastal city.

Apart from his written works, Chris Epting has ventured into television hosting and production. His popular program *Hidden Huntington Beach* uncovers the lesser-known stories and hidden gems of the city, showcasing its unique charm and history. Epting's dedication to preserving and promoting local heritage extends further through his involvement in organizations such as the Orange County Historical Commission and his advisory board membership for the Bolsa Chica Conservancy.

With his passion for storytelling and commitment to preserving the history and culture of Orange County, Chris Epting has made a significant impact as an author, journalist and advocate for local heritage. His works serve as valuable resources for those interested in exploring the rich tapestry of this vibrant region.

Visit us at
www.historypress.com